Dynamic D.M.

Prosperity Through Participatory Good Governance

Dynamic D.M.

Prosperity Through Participatory Good Governance

DR. HEERA LAL, IAS
KUMUD VERMA

PRABHAT PRAKASHAN

Published by

PRABHAT PRAKASHAN PVT. LTD.
4/19 Asaf Ali Road,
New Delhi-110 002 (INDIA)
e-mail: prabhatbooks@gmail.com

ISBN 978-93-5521-252-8
Dynamic D.M.
by Dr. Heera Lal, IAS and Kumud Verma

Edition
2024

Price
₹ 350 (Rupees Three Hundred Fifty Only)

Printed at
Sita Fine Arts, Delhi

Dedicated to My Respected Father

LATE SHRI RAM AJOR

Message from Hon'ble Governor of Uttar Pradesh

I am extremely happy to know that the book 'Dynamic DM' is being published by Dr. Heera Lal, IAS, which is based on his long administrative experience.

The Indian Administrative Service is the most prestigious service in the country. It is committed to serve a country like India, which is vast and full of social diversity. Since the basic unit of our development is the village, the responsibility of the administrative officer towards rural development becomes very important.

In the book Dynamic DM, Dr. Heera Lal shares his long administrative experiences. I believe that the contents published in the book will prove useful to the administrative officers and the youth joining the administrative service in future.

I congratulate Dr. Heera Lal for his diligence and also for providing excellent services to society. I extend my warm wishes for the publication of the book.

— **Anandiben Patel**
Governor, Uttar Pradesh

❑

Message from Chief Secretary

I am very happy to know that Dr. Heera Lal is publishing a book on his experiences as District Magistrate in Banda district with the title 'Dynamic DM'. At present, the District Magistrates, on the basis of their abilities and experiences, provide leadership to various divisions of district administration, which include revenue collection, law & order, developmental programs, infrastructure facilities, welfare schemes, disaster management, protocols, etc. At the core of all, this is the need for good governance. Changes have been occurring at a very fast pace since the last 7–8 years; in such a situation, the responsibility of the District Magistrates become more challenging.

I am sure that not only young civil service officers will be inspired by Dr. Heera Lal's experiences, but common people and beneficiaries will also be aware of all the challenges that a District Magistrate has to face during his tenure.

—Durga Shankar Mishra

Chief Secretary, Government of Uttar Pradesh

❑

Message from Founder & Editor-in-Chief, The Print

Dr. Heera Lal's efforts to bring prosperity to UP's Banda is a case study for good, strategic governance. It shows Lal's ability to connect with the people of Banda and bring modern solutions as district magistrate – from tackling water crisis, getting people to the voting booth or going plastic-free. I recommend this book to aspiring civil servants.

—Shekhar Gupta

Founder & Editor-in-Chief, The Print

❑

Foreword

First of all, congratulations on the excellent work. I have worked with many officers in my 38 years of administrative life, but I found that the author of this book, Dr. Heera Lal, possesses a different mindset. Dr. Heera Lal continuously updates his knowledge. It is his constant endeavour that new experiments for good governance should be carried out and that the common people should benefit more and more. In this book, the author has especially described the experiments carried out during his tenure as District Magistrate, Banda. Surely Dr. Heera Lal has been a 'Dynamic DM'.

At the beginning of the book, the author has described his pre-commissioning in Provincial Civil Service (PCS) which makes it clear that since childhood, he had a longing to read, write and acquire knowledge. His willpower was also strong, and he completed whatever he decided to do. The most important example was his education in America, which he completed despite many obstacles. Dr. Heera Lal has clearly written in his book that after joining the civil services, officers tend to stop reading and writing; the reason for this is that they are very busy. I agree with the fact stated by Dr. Heera Lal that the officers should keep studying continuously by taking out time so that their knowledge continues to grow, and they have relevant information at all times. Especially, this is much needed in IAS CADRE as the officers keep getting posted in different positions. Sometimes, they are District Magistrates and sometimes, they are posted in different departments in the secretariat. Therefore, it is very important for them to keep increasing and updating their knowledge in different subjects, only then will they be able to work and fulfil responsibilities efficiently. Nowadays, new challenges keep coming up in the administration. To face them, the officer has to get information about different subjects. I found that Dr. Heera Lal is a very well-read and tries his best to deliver quality by bringing new thoughts to the administration.

The post of District Magistrate is a very powerful and challenging post in itself. It is the desire of every IAS officer that he should be posted as District Magistrate so that by working on that post, they can do creditable work for their district. The district magistrate has an important role in the administration because it is the responsibility of the District Magistrate to implement the plans of all the departments at the district level. Maintaining peace in the district and working on every aspect of development is the hallmark of a good district magistrate. Unparalleled leadership ability is required to work in this position. The people and administration of the entire district function according to the working style of the district magistrate and they also have expectations. The District Magistrate has direct communication with the citizens of his district and this is the reason that every person in the district expects the District Magistrate will solve his/her problems. Even today, if there is any problem in the district, the person wants to go to the District Magistrate and present the problem to him, having full faith that his/her problem will be solved and justice will be given. The author has specifically mentioned this in his book.

I have served as the District Magistrate of Banda for some time, so I have knowledge of the problems of this district. I would like to say that Dr. Heera Lal defined the development priorities of this district in a very efficient manner and also fulfilled them with public participation.

Banda is an area in Bundelkhand where availability of water poses the biggest problem. Dr. Heera Lal made this his first priority. He went from village to village and shared information about water conservation and with the cooperation of the villagers, worked to implement water-related schemes. He has done such unique work in this field that the people there still remember him. The most important thing is that he did not get any separate budget for the development work that he did in the district. For that, he coordinated with the ongoing government schemes and ensured successful implementation with public cooperation.

Apart from conserving water, Dr. Heera Lal also worked hard during the elections and displayed a different thought process. It was because of his remarkable leadership ability that more and more voters were awakened and voted in the General Election in 2019 which earned the admiration of none other than the Prime Minister of India.

The effectiveness shown by Dr. Heera Lal in strengthening democracy was appreciated by the Election Commission also. In this book, you will find that Dr. Heera Lal designed different types of new schemes for development and implemented them in Banda district. Indeed, he was the District Magistrate of the people.

The measure of success of any District Magistrate is how much the public appreciates his work. Dr. Heera Lal has lived up to the expectation and even today in Banda district, the public praises him for the work that he did and remembers him as a District Magistrate with a difference. If this type of work is done by every District Magistrate and in the same spirit, then the real development of other districts of Uttar Pradesh will also be done certainly.

It is a matter of pleasure that many years are still left for Dr. Heera Lal to retire. I hope that he will get opportunities to work in other districts too and he will present proof of good governance with his wonderful working style and creative approach. My best wishes are with Dr. Heera Lal.

—**Alok Ranjan,** IAS (Retd.)
Former Chief Secretary, Government of Uttar Pradesh

❑

Acknowledgements

Many thanks to all of you who have directly or indirectly supported me in accomplishing the task of writing this book. It is because of your cooperation that this book has been able to see the light of the day. Had you not cooperated in the work carried out by me in Banda district, perhaps this book would not have been completed.

I have no words to express my gratitude to you. I thank you wholeheartedly again for your love, affection, cooperation and wish you all the best for your bright future. I take this opportunity to recall the names of all the colleagues and well-wishers who were instrumental for this task at the beginning itself.

Shri Shani Kumar, District Science Club, Banda and Shri Arpit Gupta, E-lets Technomedia, Lucknow played an important role in the Start-up Innovation program in the Banda district.

It is only because of the cooperation extended by Shri Rahul Verma, Political Expert, Shri Chandra Mishra, Political Expert, Shri Anil Sharma, ADR, Lucknow and Shri Shyam Nigam, Bundelkhand Connect for increasing 90+ per cent voting in the Lok Sabha General Election 2019 of Uttar Pradesh that the Banda district got the award for. I am especially grateful to you all for this.

Mr Sanjeev Kumar Baghel, District Program Officer, Banda, Mr Amit Malhotra, State Head, UNICEF, Mrs Garima Singh, Divisional Coordinator, UNICEF, Mr Yakub Muzaffar, Divisional

Coordinator, UNICEF and Mr Lekhchandra Tripathi, UNICEF provided support to expedite efforts to eradicate malnutrition in Banda district.

Shri R. K. Singh, Superintendent, District Prisons played an important role in making Banda jail the best prison of the State while supporting the prison reform program under my leadership. Banda jail received the *'Tinka-Tinka'* award for prison reforms. The full cooperation by Ms Vartika Nanda added value to this work.

The cooperation of Mr Sanjay Aggarwal, Divisional Forest Officer, Banda and Mr Junaid Ahmed, Forest Ranger, Banda in taking the *'Ped Jiao Abhiyan'* being run in the district to the public was remarkable.

Dr P. R. Verma, District Ayurvedic and Unani Officer, Banda, Dr Rajesh Rajput, Medical Officer, Banda, Shri Ramesh Singh Rajput, Yoga Teacher and Shri Ramesh Patel made commendable contributions in executing the yoga program being run in schools and colleges in the district with the objective of 'prevention is better than cure'.

Invaluable contribution was made by Shri Mithlesh Pandey, Principal, Adarsh Bajrang Inter College, Banda, and Shri Anmol, Prayatna Coaching Institute, Lucknow, in the Chhatra Nirman Samvad program run for the students of Banda district to make them aware of their goal setting.

Mr Parvez Ahmed, District Horticulture Officer, Banda, Dr Sanjay Kumar Yadav, District Panchayat Raj Officer, Banda, Shri Virendra Babu Dixit, Assistant Commissioner, Cooperatives, Dr Pramod Kumar, District Agriculture Officer, Banda and Mr Prem Singh, a progressive farmer, assisted in the Gyanarjan Yatra programme being run in Banda district for the development of the students and to enhance their talent.

Mr. Kaushalendra Singh, Assistant Director, Employment, Banda, Mr. R. K. Jain, Assistant Director, savings, Banda, Mr. Abhishek Singh, Coordinator/Vice Principal, (GIC, Banda), and Mr Yogesh Tiwari, Lecturer, economics, assisted in *'Ek Din ka Adhikari'* program organized for imparting practical knowledge and information on how the office is run to the students apart from theoretical study.

Shri R. P. Mishra, Project Officer, District Rural Agency, Banda, Shri Pramod Kumar Mishra, Assistant Engineer, Minor Irrigation, Banda, Shri Pushpendra Bhai, Apna Talab, Shri Umashankar Pandey, Jakhni, Shri Shishir, Water Aid and Km. Prashansa Gupta played an important role in propagating the Banda model of water conservation to reduce the misuse of water and manage water from ponds and rivers and for the common man to conserve rainwater. The Banda model of water conservation became an example for other districts due to the wholehearted cooperation extended by all the above people in solving the water problem in the district.

Unparalleled support was provided by Shri Pradeep Kumar, City Magistrate, Mr. Ajit Kumar, designated officer, Smt. Sarita Singh, Joint Commissioner, Commercial Tax, Shri Amit Seth Bholu and Shri Manoj Jain in the *'Jhola-yukt, plastic-mukt Banda programme'* run with the aim of making Banda plastic-free.

Shri Awadhesh Nigam, Tehsildar, Banda played an important role in the *'Neki ki Deevar ki ek anokhi pahal'* programme run with the aim of making the extra and useful clothes/accessories available to the helpless/needy and poor people to render social service to the public. For this, I am sincerely grateful to him.

Dr. Pramod Kumar, District Agriculture Officer, Banda assisted in the 'Kisan Vikas Tour program' run with the aim of doubling the income of the farmers.

It is noteworthy that special support was given in the 'Basic Education Innovation Program' run by Shri Harishchandra Nath,

District Basic Education Officer, Banda in the Basic Education Department.

A commendable contribution was made by Sri A. K. Singh, Deputy Director, Agriculture Department, Banda, Shri Ram Kumar Mathur, Land Conservation Officer, Shri Shailendra Verma, Land Conservation Officer, and Shri Saurabh Kumar, Land Conservation Officer in the grand organization of the Arhar Conference on World Oilseeds Day by branding local agricultural products under my leadership.

Administrative and District Officers in all the programs run during my tenure in Banda district viz. Shri Hira Lal, retired Chief Development Officer, Shri Harishchandra, Chief Development Officer, Shri Santosh Bahadur Singh, Additional District Magistrate (F/R) Shri Sanjay Kumar, Additional District Magistrate (Judicial), Ms. Thamim Ansaria, Joint Magistrate, Mr. Pradeep Kumar Singh, Municipal Magistrate, Ms. Vandita Srivastava, SDM, Naraini, Mr. Sandeep Kumar, SDM, Mr. Aurobindo Kumar Tiwari, SDM, Baberu, Mr. Saurabh Shukla, SDM, Atarra, Mr. Rakesh Kumar, SDM, Pailani, Mr. Mansoor Ahmed, SDM, Pailani, Mr. Mahendra Pratap, SDM, Pailani, Mr Ramkumar, Sub-Collector, Pailani, Mr. Sushil Kumar Singh, Tehsildar, Atarra/Naraini, Mr. Awadhesh Nigam, Tehsildar, Banda, Mr. Ramdayal Raman, Tehsildar, Pailani, Mr. Rajiv Nigam, Tehsildar, Pailani, Mr. Vipin Kumar, Tehsildar, Baberu, Mr. Rajesh Kumar Yadav, Naib Tehsildar, Pailani, Mr. Gyanendra Kumar Trivedi, District Development Officer, Mr. K. K. Pandey, Deputy Commissioner, NRLM, Mr. R. P. Mishra, Project Director, District Rural Development Agency, Mr. Sanjay Kumar Yadav, District Panchayati Raj Officer, Mr. Birendra Babu Dixit, Assistant Commissioner, Cooperative, Dr. Pramod Kumar, District Agriculture Officer, Mr. Ramsharan Prajapati, Deputy Dairy Development Officer, Mr. Manoj Kumar Singh, Block Development Officer, Naraini/ Bisanda, Mr. Sanjeev Kumar, Baghel, District Economics and

Numbers Officer, Banda/Block Development Officer, Mahua, Dr Prabhat Kumar Dwivedi, Block Development Officer, Kamasin/ Baberu, Mrs. Priyanka Shukla, District Training Officer, Banda/ Block Development Officer, Badokhurd, Mr. Vedprakash Maurya, Deputy Commissioner, MNREGA Banda/Block Development Officer, Jaspura, Mr. Piyush Srivastava, Block Development Officer, Tindwari, Mr. R. K. Singh, Superintendent, District Jail, Mr. Sanjay Agarwal, Divisional Forest Officer, Dr P. R. Verma, District Ayurvedic and Unani Officer, Dr Rajesh Rajput, Medical Officer, Mr Parvez Ahmed, District Horticulture Officer, Ms. Sarita Singh, Joint Commissioner, Commercial Tax, and Mr. Harishchandra Nath, the District Basic Education Officer, provided full support in the programs related to their respective work areas, as a result of which all the schemes and other programs of the government were implemented in an effective and planned manner, all the programs were completed in the stipulated time, and the people of Banda could be benefited. I will always be grateful for the commendable contribution made by all the administrative and district officers.

Journalists and media play an important role in making any program accessible to the public. Without their cooperation, it is a difficult task to implement the program and reach the common man. Shri Abdul Rashid Siddiqui, Dainik Amar Ujala, Shri Abhay Kumar Nigam, Doordarshan Channel, Shri Vimal Pandey, Dainik Jagran, Kanpur, Shri Shekhar Dwivedi, Dainik Hindustan, Kanpur, Shri Basant Gupta, Dainik Jagran, Jhansi, Shri Hardev Tripathi, Dainik National Sahara, Kanpur, Shri O. P. Tripathi, Dainik Bhaskar, Chhatarpur (MP), Shri Om Tiwari, Dainik Lok Bharti, Kanpur and Shri Prakash Gupta, Dainik Jagran, Jhansi—all of them promoted my new programs in Banda so that the government and the public continued to receive information about all the programs and the district magistrate, Banda always remained in the headlines due to their unstinted important cooperation. Your work is commendable. I not only hope but have full confidence that you will continue to provide such support in future, too. Many thanks to all of you once again. Last but not the least any omission in recollecting the names is entirely unintentional and inadvertent and my apology for that. ❑

Special Gratitudes

I would like to especially thank Mr. Umashankar Yadav, Founder Director, Ahmedabad International Literature Festival. Mr. Yadav has a rich knowledge of Hindi, English and Gujarati languages and has a keen interest in literature, art and culture. His encouragement made me to write this book. Despite being busy, he devoted his valuable time for correcting the errors and suggested many other things. I will always be grateful for the cooperation extended by Shri Umashankar Yadav.

Shri Devendra Singh Negi, Secretarial Assistant, Additional Mission Director, NHM/SIFPSA and Shri Saurabh Singh, Computer Literate Steno, Additional Project Director, Uttar Pradesh State AIDS Control Society, contributed wholeheartedly to the writing of this book. I sincerely thanks both of them.

My family is my honour and pride. My wife Dr. Usha Gangwar, son Pratyush and daughter Priyal supported me in every possible way during difficult circumstances in turning my dream into reality. I thank all of them for their love and support. I am especially indebted to my parents and the village, where the foundation of my life was laid and I grew up.

I express my gratitude to Ms. Deepti Patel, Literary Agent for her support and cooperation.

Contents

1.

Early Life

In India, PM (Prime Minister), CM (Chief Minister) and DM (District Magistrate) are the three most important, powerful and influential posts. All three posts are directly connected to the general public. Power and social prestige are closely associated with these three positions. When a poor, ordinary person from rural background and backward village reaches the topmost position like DM his fortune suddenly gets unprecedented jump. With such a sudden change in status, most people forget the original roots of their life and develop a bloated ego. A DM can use the post to improve people's lives. This is what has been done by DM Dr. Heera Lal, the main character of this book. By taking everyone along and channelising the energy Dr. Heera Lal made everyone's life better and happier.

Progress is a natural urge of every living being. Sometimes it arises from pain, sometimes from dreams and sometimes from both. Social, economic and many other circumstances are responsible for moulding someone's life. When a child comes into this world, he naturally starts adapting the environment around him/her. In this process, he/she derives pleasure from some activities, and in some cases, he/she begins to feel the pain and dreams of dealing with them. At times, the thoughts and feelings get ensconced so deep that the child starts choosing his ideals as he/she grows up. These are the ideals which envision a society which is free from all kinds of evils and ills.

Changes occur from time to time. People with conviction and determination make their own path without encountering any kind of confusion or trouble. The story of my life is also the same.

I was born in Bagdeeh village of Saughat block of Basti district in Uttar Pradesh. The ancestral occupation of my family is agriculture. My father was also employed as a compounder in the veterinary hospital, along with doing agriculture.

India lives in villages. At the time of my birth in 1966 in the village, the male child used to be given more preference in the society and family. Because of this mindset and feeling, I became the hope of the whole family. The members of the family started looking at me as a torch-bearer for its development and progress.

From 1966–1980, i.e., till class 8, I spent my childhood in the village. We had an old nice tile-roofed house. My great grandfather Late Shri Khelawan had three sons viz., Shri Lekhraj, Shri Ram Manog and Shri Ram Lagan. Shri Ram Manog was my grandfather. Shri Lekhraj and Shri Ram Lagan the other two siblings of my great grandfather had no children. Shri Ram Manog had three sons— Shri Ram Ajor, Shri Ram Prasad and Shri Nebbu Lal. My father Shri Ram Ajor has three sons—Arun Kumar, Lal Chand and me. My father Shri Ram Ajor and one of my uncle Shri Ram Prasad is no more and my other uncle Shri Nebbu Lal is with us.

I was very close to my elder Baba grandfather Shri. Lekhraj. He used to take me for a ride on bicycle. Whenever he would go out, he would definitely bring eatables for me. If he didn't bring it, I would get upset with him. So, he would explain to me why he couldn't bring it. He would make my displeasure vanish by telling me the reason for not bringing it.

My grandfather, Mr. Ram Manog was very gentle and benevolent. Sometimes on sensing the arrival of storm in the village, he used to run through the village and ask people to extinguish the fire of the hearths/stoves etc. so that the village could be saved from catching fire due to the storm. In the village, cooking with rice husk and cow dung on the earthen stove and making butter milk was in vogue.

My family was the most prosperous and respected in the village. We had a pucca (tiled) well. More than half of the village used to fetch water from it. In summer, everyone used to clean it collectively. During weddings, grooms would go round the well and light a lamp of flour and drop it in the well. It was considered auspicious. It was a 'wedding well'. Sometimes there was a lack of money too. I have also experienced lack of money at times. Sometimes I wanted to eat something, but due to paucity of money, it was either not made available or was less in quantity. I have not experienced poverty as such, but I have seen and experienced the occasional lack of money.

I am called 'Pappu' at home. I was named 'Hakim' by my family priest. I lived in Bagdeeh village from 1966 to 1980 and studied in Government Inter College Basti from 1980 to 1984. Thereafter, I studied in Allahabad for one year. From 1985 to 1990, I studied at Pantnagar University, Udham Singh Nagar (Uttarakhand). I stayed in Delhi for a year and did my preparations for civil services. In the year 1991, I took admission for M. Tech in IT BHU. I stayed in Varanasi from 1991 to 1993. From March 1993 to July 1994, I worked as an engineer in NTPC. From July 1994 to June 2016, I worked as a PCS officer. I was promoted as IAS in June 2016. I am serving in that capacity since then.

In my childhood, I was less interested in studies and more interested in playing like other children. I was scared of my father, too. Many times, I was even beaten for mistakes. During summers,

I would spend my time on the cots lying behind the house, under the trees, without even a mattress. The cool wind and the shade of the tree would work as a cooler. There was a big pond in the village. All the children would stay in the water for 2–3 hours during the noon time in summer. It was a lot of fun. My father built a pucca house by demolishing the big tile-roofed house that had been built by Baba. For that, bricks were brought from far away. I also used to carry them. Sometimes we also worked in the fields. I have a good knowledge about agriculture. I am fully aware of the plight of the farmer and how the Lekhpal (Village Revenue Officer), police and other personnel deal with the villagers and what problems the villagers face.

My father will not give me money to buy things and food during the afternoon break in school. I sometimes used to steal money from my father's trousers for these expenses. Sometimes I was caught red-handed and was scolded or at times even beaten up by my father. My father used to smoke. I was attracted to it, too. As a child, there is a natural desire to imitate and experiment. But as I was scared of my father, I used to occasionally try it secretly.

Once, there was a dispute about a wall on the way to my house. I also helped the inspector's son, who was looking into the matter, in the examination. Whatever question he asked, I would give the answer in writing. I never felt shortage of money in childhood; I lived a normal life. In the year 1978, when the house got electricity connection for the first time, we were very happy. We could run a motor of 5 horsepower for irrigation. Earlier, I used to study with a kerosene lantern or by making a lamp from a medicine bottle.

My village is on the road from Basti to Mehdawal. It is known as 'Basti-Mehdawal Road'. My village is 8 km away from Basti, and 1 km away from this road. The link road to my village was narrow and bumpy. There were many potholes on the road. Vehicles had to be driven slowly. The village was connected by a road made of mud. The roads would get slushy in rains. It was very difficult to travel. There were four settlements constituting the village. All the people were associated with farming. The people of the village had no specific thoughts and no dreams. Mohd. Amin Uncle from my village became PO in the Central Bank after doing BSc (Agriculture). Shri Uday Shankar Choudhary was a primary teacher. My father was a veterinary compounder. Thus, only three people were employed and rest of the villagers were agriculturist. Most of the houses were thatched and some were tiled. There were no pucca houses. The village was backward.

In my house, grandfather had a bicycle. Sometimes I would dismantle it completely. I would separate each one of its part. I was afraid that I would forget while reassembling the parts. Now I realise that this is how the technical mindset was formed in childhood. At that time, it was a game for me—though a risky one. As mentioned earlier, ours was the most prosperous family in the village. During those days, Ramlila used to be played in winter in the Lohroli village which was 4 km away. We were not allowed to go to Ramlila. However, we would stealthily keep clothes inside the quilt thus creating a figure of a sleeping person and slip away. We would leave in groups and return at five o'clock in the morning and then sleep. Sometimes we used to get caught. In Ramlila, we used to like the character of the joker the most.

Everyone used to help each other in building thatched houses and weddings in the village. The love and affection of the villagers for each other were worth seeing. If someone's house caught fire, then the whole village would run to douse the fire. When someone died in the village, the whole village would grieve. The atmosphere in the village was full of mutual harmony and cooperation. Absence of infrastructure and lack of information were the biggest obstacles in the development of the village. People had no dreams. The urge to move forward was also rarely seen; it was almost not there.

There is a desire for a good job in the village. It is the desire of the parents even more than the child to see their child in a good position. By the time the child is grown up, the parents start dreaming of a bright future for their children. The same happened in my case. My father dreamt that I should become an administrative officer and I became one.

I acquired my early education from a primary school till class 5. There was a lot of struggle. I would walk to the primary school in Sihari village which was about 3 km away from my village. We used to take jute sacks from home to sit on.

During the rainy season, the school used to be surrounded by water. Sometimes, one had to take off the trousers and walk through the knee-deep water. The roof of the school leaked in many places and because of that, we had to constantly move around. Firstly, all the children would have to clean the school premises. There would be a lunch break in the mid-day when children used to eat, sitting on the branches of trees in the garden, adjacent to the school. They also used to share food among themselves. Sometimes mid-day meal was available in the school. The whole school seemed like a family. There used to be an open environment under the open sky, which is not available now.

I was best student in studies in the class. The teacher used to check my notebook and I used to check the notebooks of other students in the class. It boosted my self-esteem and honour.

I studied from class 6 to 8 in Kisan Higher Secondary School, Rasulpur. It was an aided private school. Apart from this, there was no other school nearby. This school was 5 km away from my village. I had to walk 10 km every day. Shri Ram Milan Mishra was my class teacher. He used to teach us Hindi. We had to memorise Hindi. I was weak in Hindi.

Sometimes I was even beaten up with the stem of the behaya, a wild plant, which we were asked to bring. Sometimes I got red marks on both of my hands from the beating, but that beating encouraged me to become an IAS officer.

In class 8, I took an examination for Integrated Scholarship. In this scheme, one rural student was selected from each block. The selected student would get a scholarship of ₹ 100 per month and a hostel to stay. He would also get admission in Government Inter College, Basti. This examination took me from Saughat (village) to Government Inter College Basti (city) in class 9.

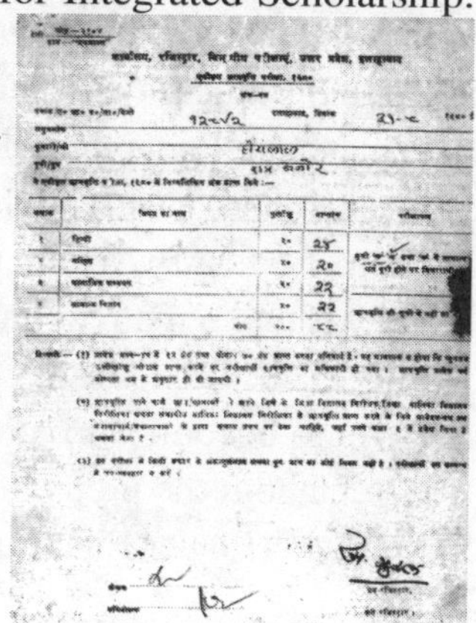

While studying in Basti, I came in contact with Shri Narendra Singh, who was the son of Hostel Superintendent Shri Dayaram Choudhary. His handwriting was captivating. I followed him and started writing as good as him.

Mr Narendra used to talk about joining the medical stream. I was impressed and started thinking to join the medical profession. But after a few months, I came in contact with Shri Shivnath Ram Gupta, an agriculture teacher. His son was studying electrical engineering at Dayal Bagh, Agra. Coming in contact with him changed my mind and made me inclined towards preparing for engineering and for this I received guidance from him. I also made up my mind to become an administrative officer after completing engineering. In class 12, Mr Dudhnath Yadav stood first and Mr Rajesh Dubey stood second. I was ranked third in the class. Both of them were selected for engineering in class 12 itself, but I was not selected. This incident brought a challenge in my life. I took admission in Allahabad University for BSc in Physics, Chemistry and Maths (PCM). I started taking coaching from Krishna Coaching. After a few months, I left BSc without informing my family members and completely focused on coaching. That decision was very difficult. I used to think that if I was not selected, then it would be very difficult. I took coaching and finally got selected. Mr Dudhnath was studying at Govind Ballabh Pant University of Agriculture and Technology in Pant Nagar. I got admission in the same University. I also joined his branch, i.e., electrical, but he was now senior to me by a year. Now in one year two room mates for four years became senior and junior. It made me feel hurt. I started my next preparation along with B.Tech. I did not have a mentor to guide me, but had a firm resolve to become an IAS officer and I kept trying. I did a lot of research about the preparation and kept studying. I got admission in M.Tech. (Power Electronics) in IT BHU by clearing the GATE Exam.

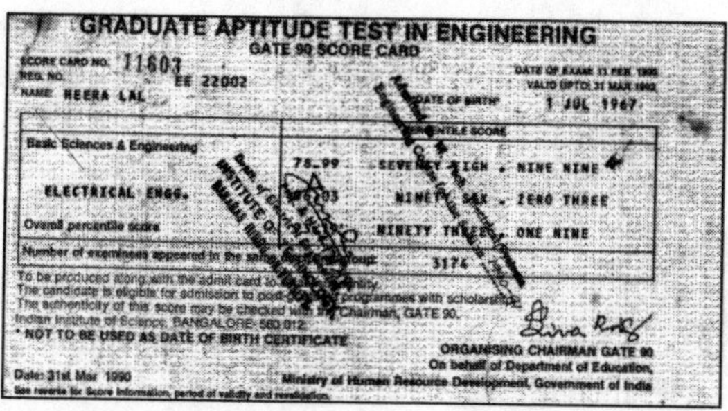

GRADUATE APTITUDE TEST IN ENGINEERING
GATE 90 SCORE CARD

SCORE CARD NO. 11603
REG. NO. EE 22002
NAME HEERA LAL
DATE OF EXAM 11 FEB 1990
VALID UPTO 31 MAR 1992
DATE OF BIRTH* 1 JUL 1967

	PERCENTILE SCORE	
Basic Sciences & Engineering	78.99	SEVENTY EIGHT . NINE NINE
ELECTRICAL ENGG.	96.03	NINETY SIX . ZERO THREE
Overall percentile score	93.19	NINETY THREE . ONE NINE
Number of examinees appeared in the same discipline group		3174

To be produced along with the admit card to ... university.
The candidate is eligible for admission to post-graduate programmes with scholarship.
The authenticity of this score may be checked with the Chairman, GATE 90.
Indian Institute of Science, BANGALORE-560 012.
* NOT TO BE USED AS DATE OF BIRTH CERTIFICATE

ORGANISING CHAIRMAN GATE 90
On behalf of Department of Education,
Ministry of Human Resource Development, Government of India

Date: 31st Mar 1990
See reverse for Score Information, period of validity and revalidation.

My aim was to prepare for civil service by getting a monthly stipend of ₹ 1,800 and availing hostel facilities so that a suitable place and environment could be found for preparation. Few other people were also preparing for civil services. There was a positive atmosphere of preparation for civil services.

Mr Amit Barnwal, a graduate from IIT Kanpur, did MTech with me. His father was a professor at IT BHU. I appeared for the IAS Main Exam for the first time, but I didn't pass. On the second attempt, I couldn't even clear the preliminary examination. Meanwhile, I had also taken the PCS exam. I got 19th rank in PCS in the very first attempt itself. I was selected in PCS from the general category. For the first time, engineering was included as the subject, and I chose electrical engineering and physics.

Shri Amit Barnwal got the third rank in the IAS in the same year. He was selected for the West Bengal cadre. Shri Amit said that it is nice if the administrative officer gets his own State. He presented many arguments. I agreed that when the person who got the third rank did not get his state, then it would be difficult for me to become an IAS in my own state.

I also had a sense of despair at not clearing the prelim. In the meantime, I got selected for the post of engineer in NTPC. I had appeared for some exams for engineering posts without any preparation. My motive was that selection would boost my morale, I would have a job in hand and the thought of unemployment would not bother me. I had decided to join PCS with the thought that after some time, I would be promoted to IAS. I completed all courses of my MTech. Only the thesis was left. By now, I was bored with my studies. The joining in PCS was late. I joined NTPC on 15 March 1993. At that time, it was a Navratna company. I joined PCS in July 1994 and was promoted to IAS on 2 June 2016 in the 2010 batch.

I still had my MTech thesis left. But now, I feel that there was no much use of studying for MTech, so why to bother about it. But after 20 years, I realised that my decision was wrong, and I should have completed MTech. So, I still regret it.

After about eight years of service, I wanted to study again. I took admission for MBA in Indira Gandhi Open University. I also appeared for some exams, but the time for studies and service as SDM didn't go well. So, I gave up my MBA course halfway. However, the seed for studies was sown in my mind. There was a scheme of the Uttar Pradesh Government that one could join a private company for three years. During that period, one would remain in the service and that half the salary would also be paid. I thought that if I could study MBA from one of the top 10 institutes of the world, then I could work in a good private company. I was the Deputy Director Mandi, Moradabad. From there, I was transferred as Additional Commissioner, Mirzapur. I didn't want to go; but after joining, I took three months' leave. I went to Ghaziabad for GMAT coaching. I stayed with my brother Mr Arun Kumar. My GMAT score was not good because there was a disconnect of twelve years with the studies. I was not too fluent in English because I had studied in Hindi medium. In my job, all the work and conversation used to be in Hindi. That's why my English language became even weaker. There was another round of urge for studies but it subsided within 6 months. However, the seed of studies was growing gradually in my consciousness.

The person who created the desire in me to go to America, is no longer in this world. I was the Sub-Divisional Magistrate (SDM) in Sambhal at that time. Ikarotiya village is in Asmauli

block of Sambhal district. Prof. Ibnul Hasan Baqri, from this village, lived in America. He had established a good school in his native village. He could never forget the struggle and hardships of his childhood. That's why Prof. Hasan opened a school in his village. He visited me once and said, "You are doing a good job as SDM. Come to America." I gradually became friends with him. I immediately took initiative in getting a passport. I had to struggle a lot to get a No Objection Certificate (NOC) for the passport. I met the then Chief Minister Hon'ble Shri Mulayam Singh Yadav and still did not get the NOC. This taught me not to withhold anyone's "No Objection Certificate". Nowadays getting an NOC has become quite easy.

At his invitation, I tried for a visa many times. But the US Embassy in India did not grant the visa. Prof. Baqri Sahib complained about this to an MP in the US. He gave a clichéd answer just like the people here. The reason was that in the wake of 9/11, visas were not granted at Muslim's invitations. I had my doubts. Otherwise, why would they not give a visa to an officer like me? The shock of being rejected twice turned visiting America into a big dream and going to America became a challenge.

This challenge was overcome with the help of a scheme of the Department of Personnel and Training, Government of India for studies abroad. All the educational expenses were borne by the Government of India, and I also received full salary. During my studies, I spent a week at Prof. Baqri's house in Florida. Prof. Baqri was a kind, good-hearted person. His entire family is in America. Even today, Prof. Baqri's indelible memory is etched in my mind. He trusted me a lot. His children, Suhail Baqri and Dr Ali Baqri, still treat me like a family, and consider me as their guardian. I have family relations with everyone of them.

I had an exceptional dream, zeal and enthusiasm to study in America. There was an atmosphere of curiosity as I was going abroad for the first time. My senior Shri Yogeshwar Ram Mishra and others had gone abroad to study. From them, I came to know that a long term training was a scheme run by the DOPT Government of India to study abroad. A long duration course of up to one year christened as Executive MPA was for the purpose of training. Earlier it was applicable only for IAS, but now PCS could also avail benefit of this scheme. Mr Mishra explained the whole process and encouraged me. I applied for it and I got selected for MPA, Syracuse University, New York, USA.

I did MPA (Master of Public Administration) from Syracuse University, USA, from August 2009 to May 2010.

I knew Mr Dipak Chandra Jain (Dean, Kellogg School of Management, USA) and I had the opportunity to visit him there. Mr Dipak Jain was the first Dean of Indian origin of the Kellogg School of Management in America.

I congratulated him on this achievement and derived inspiration from him. I was also accompanied by my BTech classmates Rajeev Agarwal and Vijay Ratnam who were living in America.

I had heard a lot about Harvard University. I had a strong desire to visit it. I also visited J. F. Kennedy School of Government situated in Chicago which was affiliated to Harvard University and the Sloan Management School affiliated to Massachusetts Institute of Technology, and learnt a lot.

I faced some difficulties in USA because of English. I surmounted this problem with the help of the English support cell. Language becomes problem for many people. Therefore, the university has established a cell for English aid. My stay in USA broadened my outlook. I got to see the world. Many of my misunderstandings were also cleared. For the first time I did everything myself for a year, but I did it happily and had fun, too. There was no provision for any servant. I cooked food for the first time in my life. Three of us stayed together. We divided the work amongst ourselves. Mr Praveen Prakash (IAS 94 AP) used to take everyone in his car for shopping. He is a very good person. We did a course together. I got an A+ and he got an A. He was very upset about it. He thought that the master was outsmarted by the disciple. Mr Praveen is a studious person. Mr Jaideep Mukherjee was the PCS of West Bengal. But all three of us stayed and studied as a family. We still have a strong relationship.

Prof. Catherine Vertini took us to visit the United Nations Headquarters in New York. Prof. Catherine was teaching there after retiring from the UN. I did two courses with her. There is a different kind of joy in studying and learning by watching; there is no boredom. I went to New York and saw the UN twice. That was a memorable moment.

After doing MPA, I came back and started my work. I developed a habit of reading and writing. I started writing blogs. I got admission in Dr. A. P. J. Abdul Kalam Technical University, Uttar Pradesh for Ph.D. in 2015 for a research topic on 'Good Governance' (Role of ICT in achieving Good Governance). I completed that in April 2020. During my PhD, I many times felt that I should give up and that I would not be able to do it. But my supporters and colleagues supported me and I completed it. Then I took admission in Dr Ram Manohar Lohia Avadh University, Ayodhya for DLitt. My research topic is 'Role of Communication in Achieving Good Governance'. Prof. Devashish Das Gupta, IIM, Lucknow and Prof. Himanshu Shekhar Singh, from Dr Ram Manohar Lohia Avadh University, Ayodhya are my guides.

I have a desire to write articles in the newspapers, but that has not been possible so far. The regret haunts me. However, I still have that desire. Reading and writing has now become a habit for me, and I enjoy it.

❑

2.

A New Phase of Life

(NTPC—from March 1993 to July 1994 PCS—from July 1994 to June 2016)

On 15 March 1993, my long-awaited dream in life came true. My first aim in life was to get a job. On the same day, I joined NTPC in Scope Complex, Lodhi Road, New Delhi. I underwent EET (Executive Engineer Training 17th Batch) training for six months at NTPC Seedhi and six months at NTPC Vindhyanagar, Madhya Pradesh. My ID No. was 06305.

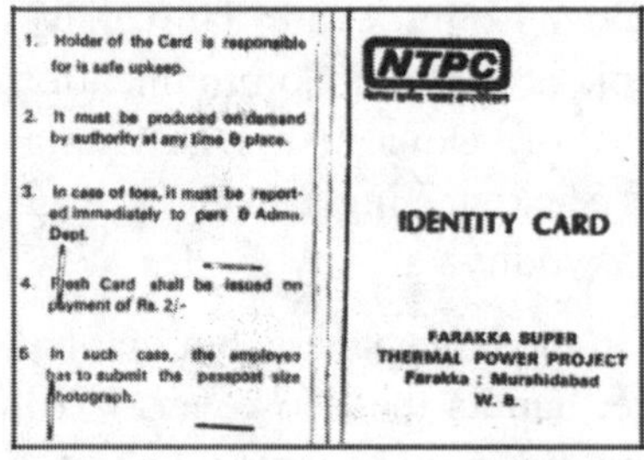
1. Holder of the Card is responsible for is safe upkeep.
2. It must be produced on demand by authority at any time & place.
3. In case of loss, it must be reported immediately to pers & Adm. Dept.
4. Fresh Card shall be issued on payment of Rs. 2/-
5. In such case, the employee has to submit the passport size photograph.

NTPC

IDENTITY CARD

FARAKKA SUPER THERMAL POWER PROJECT
Farakka : Murshidabad
W. B.

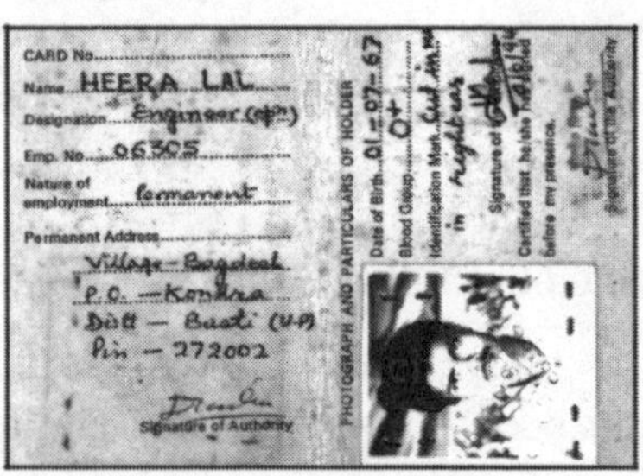
CARD No.
Name HEERA LAL
Designation Engineer
Emp. No. 06305
Nature of employment Permanent
Permanent Address
Distt — Basti (U.P.)
Pin — 272002
Signature of Authority

PHOTOGRAPH AND PARTICULARS OF HOLDER
Date of Birth 01-07-67
Blood Group O+
Identification Mark
Signature of
Certified that he/she
before my presence.
Signature of the Authority

After one year of training, I was posted as an Engineer in NTPC Farakka, West Bengal, while I was in Vindhyachal the father of my shift in-charge was admitted to NTPC hospital in Vindhyanagar. I used to take care of him. The in-charge knew that I would soon join the UP PCS. Others used to tease me thinking that I was indulging in flattery, but I took good care of him and did not bother about the taunts. Finally, one day I had to scold a fellow engineer from Orissa Mr. Mishra, and told him the truth; he was perplexed that I was selected for PCS. He realized that I am a good human being and apologised to me. When I told this to Shri R. P. Mandal, he also invited me to his house for a meal.

During the eight-hour shift in Farakka, I used to sleep on the office table during the night shift. When I went to West Bengal for the first time, I saw that the priests of the temple also eat fish. I was surprised. I came to know that they consider fish a vegetarian meal in Bengal. Fish is a staple food here. It was surprising for me.

In the first week of July 1994, I received the appointment letter duly signed by Shri Devsharan Yadav, Special Secretary, Appointment. My happiness knew no bounds. The letter had been delivered to my native place in Basti. My father sent it by the registered post to Farakka. I resigned from NTPC on 17 July 1994 and bade farewell. I underwent basic training at Nainital Academy from 19 July 1994 to 8 October 1994. I acquired practical knowledge through district training in Sultanpur district from 10 October 1994 to 4 February 1995.

In Sultanpur, Shri Iftkharuddin was the District Magistrate. I was allotted the job of City Magistrate. It was a promotion post which is given after nine years of service. The main city used to experience jams due to plying of taxis. Illegal operations of taxis existed. I tried to fix it. The vehicle of the then MLA was also a part of it. Illegal traffic operation was controlled gradually. A long existing chronic problem of traffic jam was solved. This gave good relief to common man. I earned a good name for this. I had no experience, but a huge enthusiasm. People conspired against me and even got my car hit at a cross road so that I get discouraged and stop working. The MLA complained about me to Chief Minister, Shri Mulayam Singh Yadav saying that the city magistrate asks for a vehicle and stops the vehicle if it was not given; also that he harasses the vehicle owners. The government enquired from the District Magistrate. The District Magistrate told that he lives alone and that he himself had given him the car. He also said that he is fixing the traffic system of the city and is doing a good job. I came to know of this later from the District Magistrate himself. District Magistrates often get such complex and risky tasks done by trainees because they have zero experience but are extremely energetic. The trainees do not think about pros & cons and focus on their mission. The urge for earning name by doing good work was born in me there.

The illegal operation of taxis in entire Sultanpur district and surrounding area like Allahabad, Pratapgarh, Faizabad, Ambedkar Nagar etc. where these taxis were plying to was stopped. Illicit earning was stopped. The transport officials and policemen used to tell that fix things with the City Magistrate. We can't help. It was also true that they were not fully cooperating with me. The reason for this was clear—they also had something to gain. I used to take home guards along with me for security. The home guards were good and loyal and used to keep full attention on my security.

The PCS training was of one year—three months basic, six months district training, and three months professional training. The six months of district training in Sultanpur district was memorable. The reason—(1) the stint started with my promotion to City Magistrate which used to take 9 years for a new officer. (2) I also fixed the complex problem of traffic and gained a lot of appreciation. From there, I developed the mindset of doing good work and following a right path.

After one year of training, my first posting was in Nainital district. I was given the charge of the post of Additional City Magistrate, Haldwani by the District Magistrate. Honourable Chief Minister Mayawati made a separate Udham Singh Nagar district from Nainital. The then District Magistrate Shri Praveer Kumar made me the executive Magistrate/Sub-district Magistrate of Ramnagar sub-tehsil. Earlier it was a sub-tehsil of Kashipur tehsil. Kashipur went to Udham Singh Nagar. Developing it as a pargana (sub-division of district) was a challenge. I made my residence in Kisan Bhawan of Kisan Mandi. I set up a sub–district magistrate's court/office in the Kisan Auditorium of Mandi. I took the work of tehsildar from naib tehsildar in-charge, sub-tehsil, Ramnagar. The area was always sensitive because of the VIP excursions to Jim Corbett.

One day, the Kumaon Commissioner called me to his residence in Nainital regarding a property, asking me to bring my official seal. He said that the OSD had the land-related papers and asked me to sign them. It was a typed certificate. It had to be certified in the name of the owner of a large plot of land, a well-known film actor from Bombay. I walked away under the pretext of finding out the facts. I didn't sign. I acted courageously; otherwise, I would have been in great trouble. Later that Commissioner indirectly punished me. Shri Praveer Kumar was the District Magistrate. He encouraged me and through his efforts, a new pargana was established from a sub-tehsil. Since Nagar Palika Parishad Ramnagar was dissolved, I was also the administrator. I began to visit the villages and started giving information by putting up a chaupal (community meeting place in village) and solving the problems on the spot. There, I got a chance to work independently. I worked hard and learnt a lot. My self-esteem, confidence and practical knowledge increased tremendously. That period was like an SDM internship. I also experienced the intoxication of power that one goes through in the initial phase. I got many opportunities to do fruitful work. I learnt to work in harmony with the officers with good humour and everyone's cooperation. Within a year, Ramnagar Pargana became quite famous because of its good performance. People started managing for deployment there.

I took action against a person who had illegally occupied a godown of the municipality. This man was a nefarious person and also a small-time journalist. So far, no one took action out of fear. I took action to get the Ramnagar godown vacated. Everyone got together and had me transferred using the influence of local MP

Shri Narayan Dutt Tiwari to Pithoragarh. I did not like it. I went to Lucknow and met the then Chief Secretary Shri Mata Prasad. When I showed all the facts on paper, my transfer was cancelled. At that time, the District Magistrate had changed. The new district magistrate used to praise my work, but he also wanted to remove me. The DM knew about my contacts, that's why he couldn't remove me even though he wanted too. He also applied some pressure for doing few wrong things but I did not do that. Later, the District Magistrate wrote against me. But I had evidence, so nothing happened. Therefore, if your work is good and you are popular within the public, even the District Magistrate will not be able to do anything against you. Yes, there will be some inconvenience. Through this experience, I learnt the way to deal with a unlawful and the arbitrariness of the District Magistrate.

The Garjiya temple is still ensconced in my consciousness. This temple is situated at a beautiful place on the banks of the Kosi River. A poor woman used to sit near the temple. The priest in the temple forbade the poor widow from sitting near the temple. I made the old lady to sit there, got her a ration card made and visited her house. The influential priest family became enraged, but it could not harass and drive away a helpless elderly woman. This woman had some super natural power as she used to tell something by holding rice in her hand.

The demand for a separate state of Uttarakhand was in full swing. Ramnagar was one of the main centres of this movement. Shri Prabhat Dhyani and Smt. Dhaneshwari Ghidiyal were its main leaders. I had a good rapport with everyone, due to which there was no untoward incident. I had won the trust of the public through my hard work, better coordination with the general public and good work.

After Ramnagar, Nainital, I was transferred to Barabanki. I was made the SDM of Haidergarh. I transferred the tehsildar's Ardali. The Ardali (personal help) was knowing about all the files of the tehsil's litigation cases and was in collusion with some of the touts there. Some lawyers were also involved in it. There were many complaints of corruption against the Ardali. The Ardali made all the advocates gang up against me for a strike because all the illegal earnings that the people made through him were stopped. All the advocates met the Commissioner of Faizabad. The Commissioner also asked the District Magistrate to transfer me. Meanwhile, I lodged an FIR against the MD and others in the Minor Irrigation Department scam. Regarding this, all the BDOs met the district magistrate to remove me from the post. I was removed from the post of SDM Haidergarh and attached to the headquarters as a punishment. I stayed in Haidergarh for six months. I had the image of a good officer, but I realised that I did not act as an experienced officer. I should have filed the FIR only after informing the district magistrate. I knew that if I had told her, I would not have been allowed to register the FIR. So, I filed it straightaway. But it was not the right way. I realised that later. Due to my good work in tehsil reform, the brokers acted to remove me and were successful, too. For the next six months, I worked in the headquarters as in-charge of traffic during the Lok Sabha elections. After about a year, I was transferred to Bareilly. There I was appointed the SDM, Baheri, Bareilly, by the District Magistrate Shri Sitaram Meena.

In Baheri, the private sugar mill Venus used to buy sugarcane by showing less weight and cheating the farmers. This business was going on for many years. I cross checked the complaint and found it to be true. The Venus Mill owners were very close to the then Commissioner, Bareilly Division, as earlier he was the District Magistrate, Bareilly. The Inspector of Weights & Measures was also under the influence of the mill, but I myself made a surprise

केसर मिल गेट पर घटतौली पकड़ी, रिपोर्ट दर्ज

किसानों की शिकायत पर एसडीएम ने तौल करवाई

inspection of the sugarcane purchasing centres and detected the fraud of showing less weight of the cane supplied by farmers. I got an FIR filed by the Inspector of Weights & Measures. The Commissioner was hurt more than the Venus Mill owners. The Commissioner did not have a good reputation. This boosted my morale to do good work. Its benefit was that the common sugarcane growers got acquainted with the fraudulent act of the mill. The scam got busted. The real face of the mill was exposed to the public. After this action, I was transferred out of the district, but all the local public representatives came together, and my transfer was cancelled by Chief Minister. I worked more courageously.

The name of a person that was illegally and irregularly recorded in the records relating to the precious land of Ramlila was removed. This man was also influential and a crook too. He was involved in many illegal activities. I cancelled an illegal order for 33.76 hectares of government land in the village Thana. I protected the government land by getting set aside the appeal against this order.

हीरालाल ने पथिक को कार्रवाई की परिधि में घसीटा

जागरण संवाददाता

बरेली, 25 जून। उप जिलाधिकारी बहेड़ी हीरालाल ने अपर आयुक्त न्यायिक देवशरण पथिक से पंगा मोल ले लिया है। उन्होंने जिलाधिकारी व आयुक्त को पत्र लिखकर अपर आयुक्त पर राज्य सरकार के हित के विपरीत कार्य करने का आरोप लगाया है।

पंगे की वजह बहेड़ी के परगना चौमहला के ग्राम थाना की भूमि है। इस ग्राम में 3376 हेक्टेयर भूमि पर खाता संख्या 16 में नन्दलाल सरन व उमेश कुमार के नाम अंकित थे। एसडीएम बहेड़ी हीरालाल को जब यह पता चला कि यह भूमि ग्राम समाज की है तो उन्होंने छानबीन की। जांच में पता चला कि मुकदमा नम्बर 24 सन् 68 अन्तर्गत धारा 33/39 भू-राजस्व अधिनियम के तहत 17 सितंबर 69 को तत्कालीन तहसीलदार श्रीनिवास शर्मा द्वारा इन खातेदारों के नाम दर्ज करने का आदेश पारित किया गया था। इस आदेश में सभी गाटा संख्याएं मरघट व खलियान के रूप में अंकित है और नन्दलाल सरन व उमेश कुमार का अनाधिकृत कब्जा श्रेणी-4 में दिखाया गया है और 12 वर्ष से अधिक के कब्जे को आधार मानकर सीरदार दर्ज करने के आदेश तत्कालीन तहसीलदार द्वारा दिए गये है।

❑अपर आयुक्त पर राज्य सरकार के हित के विपरीत कार्य करने का आरोप लगाया, कमिश्नर ने राजस्व परिषद में अपील दायर करने के निर्देश दिए

सूत्रों के अनुसार धारा 33/39 में यह आदेश संभव ही नही है यह कार्य धारा 229 बी जेड ए एल आर एक्ट के अन्तर्गत ही हो सकता है। तहसीलदार न्यायालय को धारा 33/39 भू राजस्व अधिनियम के अन्तर्गत कभी भी आदेश करने का अधिकार नहीं रहा है। डीजीसी राजस्व सत्येन्द्र कुमार से विधिक राय के बाद एसडीएम ने 15 सितम्बर 98 को गलत अंकित नामों को खारिज करके राज्य सरकार की विभिन्न मदों में दर्ज करने के आदेश दिए। उन्होंने तहसीलदार का आदेश शून्य माना क्योंकि यह बिना अधिकारिता के जारी किया गया था।

सूत्रों के अनुसार एसडीएम के इस आदेश के विरुद्ध नन्दलाल सरन ने अपर आयुक्त न्यायिक प्रथम देवशरण पथिक के यहां 'निगरानी' योजित की। राज्य सरकार के हित को सुरक्षित रखने का तर्क देते हुए एसडीएम ने जिलाधिकारी बरेली को पत्र लिखा कि वह मंडलीय डीजीसी राजस्व को समुचित पैरवी करने के आदेश दें। अपर आयुक्त ने निगरानी स्वीकार करके एसडीएम का आदेश खारिज कर इस पंगे को जन्म दिया। अपर आयुक्त के अनुसार धारा 33/39 भू राजस्व अधिनियम के अन्तर्गत केवल लिपिकीय त्रुटि ही संशोधित की जा सकती है। इसमें स्वत्व प्रभावित वाले आदेश स्वीकार नहीं किये जाते हैं।

सूत्रों के अनुसार अपर आयुक्त द्वारा अपने आदेश को खारिज करने से खिसियाये एसडीएम ने एक ही धारा के अन्तर्गत श्री पथिक द्वारा विरोधाभासी निर्णय खोज निकाले और उन्हें जिलाधिकारी रमारमण व मंडलायुक्त अमल कुमार वर्मा को भेज दिया। उन्होंने इस पंगे में मंडलीय शासकीय अधिवक्ता राजस्व के.सी. पाराशरी को भी शामिल किया है। श्री पाराशरी ने बहस में कई राजस्व निर्णय का उल्लेख किया था, जो राज्य सरकार के पक्ष में किन्तु निर्णय में इनका उल्लेख नही किया गया है। इस निर्णय प्रति श्री पाराशरी को पांच माह बाद मिली।

एसडीएम ने आला अफसरों को लिखे पत्र में इस मामले में सरकार के पक्ष का पूरी तरह से आकलन सही किया गया है। एसडीएम ने इस प्रकरण को अध्यक्ष राजस्व परिषद व प्रमुख सचिव राजस्व परिषद के संज्ञान में लाने का आग्रह किया है ताकि राज्य सरकार का अहित रुक सके। इस आग्रह के पीछे अपर आयुक्त के विरुद्ध कार्रवाई करवाने की मंशा है। प्रशासनिक सूत्रों के अनुसार मंडलायुक्त अमल कुमार वर्मा व जिलाधिकारी रमारमण ने इस प्रकरण में राजस्व परिषद में अपील दायर करने के निर्देश दिए है जिसकी तैयारी शुरू कर दी गई है। यह मामला तूल पकड़ने के आसार हैं, क्योंकि एसडीएम ने आरोप पर श्री पथिक भी चुप बैठने वाले नही हैं।

All the antagonistic forces united and got me transferred again. I became SDM, Sadar, Bareilly. I was moved to Moradabad district after 6 months. The two frequent transfers didn't discourage me, rather I learnt how-to do-good work in difficult situations. The Venus Mill owners had never imagined that someone with a powerful commissioner on their side would be confronted by an SDM level officer who would reveal the mill's scandal and expose it to the public. I won the hearts of the people and people appreciated me.

In Moradabad, I was appointed as SDM Sambhal. Later, after getting promoted there, I became ADM (Administration) Sambhal. The Municipal Council, Sambhal was dissolved. As an ADM, I should have been appointed the Administrator. That used to be the practice in the past. But the DM gave the charge to the SDM. One day, I went to Delhi and met local SP MP Shri Ram Gopal Yadav. On seeing me, he said, "How did the SDM get the charge?" He called someone on phone and scolded him a lot in front of me. When I returned the next day, I came to know that the DM had made me the administrator of the municipality. The former president of Municipal Council had manipulated the DM to do all of it so that her misdeeds would not be revealed. This incident came as a challenge for me. I decided to make Sambhal the number one municipality in the entire state and I did it, too. I recruited the sweepers in transparent manner. Not a single penny was spent by anyone. I did not even accept the recommendation of the District Magistrate. All the brokers and leaders of the city failed in their attempts. A good message went out in the municipal workers. A red uniform was given to everyone. I immediately deposited Rs 50 lakhs PF (Provident Fund) which was outstanding for 20 years. I used to have a meal of khichdi sitting on the floor with the sweepers, every month. Due to this, the sweepers became my fans. The city became much cleaner. Similarly, I fixed the electricity and water system. I got parks built on 26 government lands. The places where there was encroachment or dirt were converted into parks. The city was named a 'Park City'. Even today these projects are seen at the locations and speak for themselves. After my transfer, the pond which was restored after removing the encroachment was named 'Heera Kund' after my name. Five-year tax rate was revised as per the rules. The look and feel of the city changed. I was greatly appreciated for this. It really gave a good feeling when people went to the park and talked good things about me. I enhanced good governance by doing constructive and positive work through the municipality. Even today, when I think about it, energy rushes through me. For the first time, I learnt how to make a name by doing development work and how to win the hearts of the people.

There is a grand event of Muharram Tazia every year. In Sambhal, very tall Tazias (representation of tomb of Hussain) are made. It is the most sensitive festival there. Once a tall Tazia made with the collusion of the local minister and the police station in-charge could not move due to a branch of a peepal tree on the way. The people did not want the tazia to be moved by dividing it into two parts. The Hindus were not ready to cut the branch. The branch had crossed the road and gone to the other side. It was a thick branch. I suddenly received the information at eleven o'clock at night. I went to the spot with the CO. I spoke to both sides; they did not listen. Many times, the furious mob climbed on the tree and started cutting the branch. They were brought down with great effort. The news spread to the surrounding cities and districts. Everyone refused to take the Tazia forward. An atmosphere of unrest started building up all around. I started to feel that something very bad was about to happen. Due to this episode, the law and order in many districts was deteriorating. By three O'clock in the morning, the politics behind this became clear. I woke up the local minister at three O'clock and spoke to him. I clearly told him that all efforts have been made, but people are not agreeing and that I have no option but to use force. This worked for me. The key was found. After discussions over the next two hours, the Tazia was taken out in two parts and was joined again. The branch was not cut. All this was done by the local politicians who were upset with the DM and SSP to have influence on them. The DM and SSP did not arrive at the spot, though they were requested several times. When everything was set right, they arrived at five in the morning. I also saw a new method of applying pressure. Create a problem of law and order, get it resolved on request and show it as a favour. They wanted to impose a favour on the DM and SSP. I saw and learnt about the manoeuver of creating political pressure. It was a new experience.

One day, I was having lunch at 1:30 p.m. I received information on the wireless set that the Hayat Nagar SHO had been surrounded by a crowd in a case of a land dispute. There was apprehension of an unpleasant incident. I told CO Mr Harendra Yadav, left my lunch, took my revolver, loaded it and left immediately with the home guard. There was a furious crowd of around ten thousand people at the location. The two sides had come face to face at a distance of hundred metres on either side of the road. The CO had also arrived. I sent the CO on one side and on the other, I took over the entire command. With only two home guards, with a stick in one hand and a revolver in the other, I kept shouting, driving the crowd away.

In about two hours, I was able to clear the crowd from the road and send them back. The Additional Superintendent of Police kept shouting on the wireless set that he is coming. He kept giving his location. He covered the distance in two hours which should have

अमन-चैन बिगाड़ने की कोशिश

हयातनगर में पुलिस ने कराये हालात पैदा

■ समय से कार्रवाई कर देती तो पड़ोसियों के मन में नहीं पनपती खटास

दोनों सम्प्रदायों ने कहा–मसले को मिल बैठ कर निपटा लेते

taken only ten minutes. When the matter had settled down, he reached the spot and started showing off so that the media persons would take his photographs and write that the riot was stopped by the Additional Superintendent of Police. I had worked so hard running around and shouting for two hours that it took next seven days for my legs to return to normal. The Additional Superintendent of Police was an imposter and had a penchant for exaggeration. He had a flair for showing others' work as his own. The next day, my photograph with the revolver was published on the front page of all the newspapers. The title was, 'SDM prevented the riot by risking his life'. This incident made me feel like a hero. Here, my good reputation, good coordination among the general public and public's confidence in my work came in handy. Everyone knew that since the SDM had come to the spot, everything would be alright. Everyone knew that no one could influence me.

Once, I was invited as the chief guest to a school in Sambhal. At the end of the programme, a lady told me that she had FDR (Fixed Deposit Receipt) of SBI and that the bankers were not encashing it for three months. I went straight to the bank with the woman. Through on-the-spot conversation and investigation, I came to know that the FDR was fake. A bank employee had issued a fake FDR. The incident was disturbing. Slowly, the facts came to light. A clerk of the bank Shri Diwakar Agnihotri had formed a cooperative organisation of bank workers and used to deposit money through mutual cooperation. People used to make transactions according to their needs. That employee got the FDRs printed which looked like FDRs of SBI. When someone would come for a FDR in the bank, he used to give this fake FDR instead of the genuine SBI FDR. That was how he kept making money. Since the clerk of the bank was doing this within the premises of the bank, no one had any suspicions. The fake FDR also looked exactly like that of the original FDR issued by SBI. He used to cheat the innocent, less educated public.

मुरादाबाद जागरण

एसबीआई में समानांतर बैंकिंग का भंडाफोड़

फर्जी एफडीआर से गरीबों के साथ लाखों की धोखाधड़ी

एडीएम ने दिए बैंक कर्मी के खिलाफ रिपोर्ट के आदेश

Many people in the bank knew about it. He used to keep the local leader and senior officials under control by bribing them. In the past, when a manager wanted to stop him, he got him attacked. By paying bribes, he got the manager transferred. After about a month of investigation, a scam of several crores came to the fore. I wrote about this scam at every level. The media widely covered this. The money of many poor people was stuck, and the marriage of many girls could not take place. I worked with full force and took personal interest. It was completely busted. I also went and met the Finance Secretary in Delhi and gave him all the related papers. The SBI staff did not act as promptly as it should have. I was alone in this fight. The people from media fully supported me. I was able to stop further scams from happening. I wrote for the action for return of the money. I wrote to Mussoorie Academy for the case to be studied as a case study. There, it was taught and explained in the form of a case study. In this episode, helping the poor gave me self-satisfaction and I felt good.

There are two types of development—constructive development and destructive development. First, building a new school on vacant land is constructive development and second, evicting poor people who live by building houses on government-owned barren land and building schools on it is destructive development. My approach is constructive development. The main function of an Administrative Officer is constructive development. One should enjoy doing that. The post of Chief Development Officer (CDO) is the best post for constructive work. I was posted as CDO in Ballia, I did not join for 15 days. There were many negative apprehensions in my mind about Ballia, but there was pressure from the government that my transfer would not be cancelled. I was forced to join. Poverty was rampant in Ballia. I found the development of the district poor. Ballia is on the border of Bihar. Therefore, most of the business and kinship here is with Bihar. I felt that its attachment was more to Bihar and less to Uttar Pradesh.

जिले ने दिया सम्मान: सीडीओ

बलिया। जिले के चर्चित मुख्य विकास अधिकारी हीरालाल का स्थानांतरण फिरोजाबाद के लिए हो गया। स्थानांतरण की सूचना मिलते ही विकास भवन के अधिकारी, कर्मचारी एवं उनके शुभचिन्तकों की भीड़ शुक्रवार को उनके आवास पर जुट गई। भीड़ को देखकर सीडीओ भावकु हो गये। कहा कि बलिया जिले में कर्मचारियों ने जो सम्मान मुझे दिया है उसे सदैव याद रखूंगा। मेरे काम करने की शैली में कर्मचारियों की भी अहम भूमिका रही है। जहां भी रहूंगा बलिया की याद आती रहेगी। इस दौरान मुख्य चिकित्सा अधिकारी डा. मंसूर अहमद, एनआरएचएम के जिला कार्यक्रम प्रबंधक मनोज कुमार, डीपीआरओ घनश्याम सागर, पीडी प्रमोद यादव, पिछड़ा वर्ग कल्याण अधिकारी नरेन्द्र शर्मा सहित अन्य अधिकारी एवं कर्मचारियों ने बुके देकर सम्मानित किया। इसके बाद सीडीओ ने सूचना विभाग के देशदीपक यादव को प्रशस्ति पत्र देकर सम्मानित किया। कहा कि श्री यादव की प्रचार-प्रसार में अहम भूमिका रही है और समाचार संकलन में भी विशेष योगदान रहा है। उन्होंने पीठ थपथपाते हुए इसके लिए श्री यादव को बधाई दी। इस अवसर पर गौरीशंकर राय, सच्चिदानंद दूबे, सीताराम सिंह, कामेश्वर उपाध्याय, अवधेश चौरसिया, इसरार अहमद, शैलेश ओझा आदि मौजूद रहे।

सीडीओ हीरालाल को विदाई देते सीएमओ डा. मंसूर अहमद, सूचना विभाग के देशदीपक यादव को सम्मानित करते सीडीओ हीरालाल

I worked hard. This was my first posting as CDO. I had no experience in this position. I awakened, alerted and stirred all the functionaries through study and careful monitoring. This led to progress in work. The bad work culture began to improve. There was a stir in the sluggish district administration. Everyone started working hard and efforts increased. The bad image began to fade away and a good image began to form. Here, I learnt a lot as a CDO probationer. From the hospital to the school, I used to keep a close watch on everyone. Due to good work, a public representative who knew me got me transferred as CDO Firozabad because his son wanted to contest the forthcoming election of Member of Parliament.

A scam of mid-day meal came to light in Firozabad. Three NGOs were supplying mid-day meals till five years back. A year later, only Saraswat Shiksha Seva Samiti got this project and the other two did not.

The CBI was investigating the mid-day meal scam in the neighbouring district of Mainpuri. The news of this scam was scary. This was a five-year-old matter. Shri Chandrakant Sharma was a primary teacher. At the same time, he was running NGOs by other names. His father was also a teacher. Two FIRs were registered against him. He had also gone to jail. Former BSA Altaf told me that he had also suspended him. He was known as a 'mafia' in the department. He used to earn money through the mid-day meal scam. He had clout due to money and political nexus. When his file came to me for renewal of contract, I started looking through it and caught the misdeed. Many former BSAs and high officials were also involved in this. They bypassed me and got the renewal done by the then District Magistrate. Shri Chandrakant Sharma had made a very close relative of his, office-bearer in the organisation, but he used to do everything himself. He had command over the department. The members of the enquiry committee signed the inquiry report reluctantly because of the fear of Sharma. During the investigation, many former District Magistrates and Chief Development Officers and Basic Education Officers also sent their favorable recommendations. There was also pressure not to carry out the investigation. Finally, in my place, the district magistrate conducted the inquiry under his chairmanship. Shri Chandrakant Sharma was punished. A basic education officer was also punished. District Magistrate Shri Vijay Kiran Anand supported me in bringing the scam to the end. The then Chief

Treasury Officer (CTO) Shri Pushpraj Saxena played an important role in this investigation. Subsequently four NGOs were selected in a transparent manner. A five-year-long scandal came to an end. I had to go through trouble many times during this good work.

The former high officials were upset, but I got the thieves of the children's food punished, and the theft stopped.

अमर उजाला अपना फीरोजाबाद 3

जांच की आंच: घोटालों में फंसी कई की गर्दन

फाइलों में उलझ गई एमडीएम संस्था की जांच

बीडीओ के खिलाफ जांच कमेटी गठित

प्रधान और सचिव अंतिम जांच में दोषी

डीपीआरओ के फर्जी हस्ताक्षर से निकाला

Shri Gangaram Verma was a BDO through direct recruitment. No one wanted to take him as the block chief because he was honest and law-abiding. There was also a shortage of BDOs. Many BDO were in charge of more than two blocks. Shri M. P. Prabal who was promoted from ADO to BDO was in high demand. He was in charge of upto three blocks. The block chiefs create so much controversy that the whole work gets embroiled in a dispute. Therefore, care has to be taken that there is no disturbance, and the work goes smoothly. Mr Prabal worked with me for a few months. Due to his being in the district for a long time, he was transferred to Gonda district in view of the elections.

One day, I went to inspect a block. The CDO is required to inspect the blocks. I came to know that the payment for signboards in MGNREGA had been made, but the boards had not been installed on the spot. It was proved after going through the papers of many village secretaries. All this had happened during the tenure of Mr Prabal. I got a committee constituted by the district magistrate for a thorough and in-depth investigation. This scam came to the fore in the report. The DM wrote a letter for action against the then BDO Shri Prabal.

सीडीओ ने पूर्व बीडीओ के खिलाफ बैठाई जांच

फीरोजाबाद: मनरेगा योजना से साइन बोर्ड लगाने के नाम पर लाखों रुपए का घपला करने के आरोप में मुख्य विकास अधिकारी ने जिले में तैनात रहे एक खंड विकास अधिकारी के खिलाफ जांच शुरू कर दी है। एक टीम गठित कर सात दिन में रिपोर्ट देने को कहा गया है। सीडीओ हीरा लाल ने गुरुवार को एका ब्लॉक का निरीक्षण किया था। इस दौरान उन्हें पता चला कि एका में तैनात रहे बीडीओ एमपी प्रबल के कार्यकाल में मनरेगा से कुछ साइन बोर्ड खरीदे गए थे, लेकिन वास्तव में कहीं कोई बोर्ड नहीं लगे। हालांकि बोर्ड के नाम पर भुगतान कर दिया गया। ब्लॉक खैरगढ़ में भी उन्हें इस तरह की शिकायत मिली कि बिना बोर्ड लगे

• मनरेगा से साइन बोर्ड लगाने के नाम पर घपले का आरोप

ही बीडीओ ने ग्राम पंचायत अधिकारी के माध्यम से कुछ बोर्ड का भुगतान करा दिया। सीडीओ ने बताया कि ये सीधे सीधे मनरेगा में घपला और धनराशि के दुरुपयोग का मामला है।

इसलिए बीडीओ एमपी प्रबल के खिलाफ जांच शुरू करा दी गई है। डीएम के निर्देश पर एक टीम गठित की गई है। जिसमें पीडी डीआरडीए सर्वेश चंद यादव, डीडीओ आरके राम और आरइएस के सहायक अभियंता को शामिल किया गया है। ये टीम उन सभी ब्लॉकों में एमपी प्रबल द्वारा कराए गए कार्यों की जांच करेगी, जो उन्होंने अपने कार्यकाल में किए हैं। उल्लेखनीय है कि वर्तमान में गौंडा जिले में तैनात बीडीओ एमपी प्रबल जिले के फीरोजाबाद, शिकोहाबाद, खैरगढ़, एका व नारखी में तैनात रहे थे।

पूर्वाग्रह से ग्रसित: प्रबल

इस मामले में पूर्व बीडीओ एमपी प्रबल का कहना है कि सीडीओ उनके खिलाफ द्वेष भावना से कार्य कर रहे हैं। उन्होंने सीडीओ की शिकायत प्रमुख सचिव ग्राम्य विकास, पुलिस महानिदेशक और एससीएसटी आयोग से की है।

After a few months, I was transferred from Firozabad to Special Secretary, Home Guard, Lucknow. About four months after I reached Lucknow, I received an order from Gonda CJM about filing a suit against me. This suit was filed by Mr Prabal. He had cooked up the story that I went to Gonda twice, abused and thrashed him in his campus. Mr Prabal gave a complaint to the police. The case was not registered. Therefore, he got the CJM court order to file a case. All the notices were made by showing fake execution. I appealed to the district judge against the order of the CJM court. I attached all the documents written against him as evidence. I was in Lucknow at the time of the incident, and I proved that with the location on my mobile.

मनरेगा के बोर्ड लगे नहीं, धनराशि निकाली

निरीक्षण

- पूर्व बीडीओ पर 87 हजार के घोटाले की जांच को सीडीओ ने समिति गठित की
- कार्यकाल के दौरान किए गए सभी कार्यों की जांच होगी

लाखों का घपला सामने आने की संभावना

जांच कमेटी में ये शामिल

यहां होंगी जांचें

CJM's order was quashed. Upset with the action of the MGNREGA board, Mr. Prabal had concocted a story against me and forged papers. The court also did not look closely at them with issued the order. Shri Prabal retired from Gonda. He was punished. His strength was earning money illegally and distributing it; that is why everyone liked him. Most of the elected heads of the blocks wanted him to be their BDO. Mr Prabal applied the same fake formula to me, too, but this time he was trapped. When you want to do good work, you might face trouble. The same happened with me, too.

My experience has been that you have to suffer for your good and just work. The trouble of doing good work brings with it, joy and experience. You get to learn a lot. Your strength increases. It is our main responsibility to win justice in the face of injustice and to bring smiles on the faces of the people. If we tell the truth in a logical way along with evidence, then people believe it. For this, you have to go through all kinds of troubles. One has to go through test from time to time, but eventually, he wins. One's experience grows and self-confidence becomes very strong. Such struggle during service enhances the personality and increases the strength of the person. After recovering from the trouble, the feeling of victory appears automatically.

❑

3.

Dynamic DM

Why is the book titled 'Dynamic DM'?

The literal meaning of dynamic is active, moving, energy, and replete with various thoughts. During my tenure as DM in Banda, people saw all these elements in me, and the public, media and other people in the government department started addressing me by the nickname of 'Dynamic DM'.

After a long time, the public and the media saw a district magistrate who was putting in hard work, relentlessly implementing programmes, was passionate and running around. Seeing all this, people simply started calling me 'Dynamic DM'.

This nickname started being used in meetings, programmes, etc. Bundelkhand News created a video of 8:07 minutes on 5 December 2019. Its title was 'Dynamic DM'. Banda DM Heera Lal is really 'Dynamic'. This video is available online at this news site—www.bundelkhandnews.com.

This book has been named on the above basis. The people of Banda have given me this name. In this book, I have made an attempt to cover all kinds of sweet and sour experiences of my journey from Basti to Banda.

बाँदा जागरण

जनपद में विकास के डेढ़ साल, बेमिसाल

पूर्व डीएम ने जिले के लिए हर क्षेत्र में बढ़ाए कदम

आमजन के बीच सक्रियता ने उन्हें बनाया था डायनेमिक डीएम

ध्यान से लेकर मतदान तक हर तरफ छाए रहे काम

आम के साथ खास लोग भी कहते हैं डायनेमिक डीएम

Through this book, I thought it appropriate to live those moments and communicate my work to the readers and pen them down with this name. Although people had different views on this but I found the word 'dynamic' to be more of a noun than an adjective. If I had given another name, I think that this book might not have had much relevance.

The zeal to do something different and work in the interest of the public was so much a part of me that during my entire tenure, I lived mostly in the field, with and among the people of the district. That's probably the story of Dynamic DM.

The posts of PM, CM and DM are the best and most suitable for serving the society in India. These three positions are powerful, prestigious, dignified, and full of challenges. They change the direction and condition of the country, state and district respectively and make them better. They strengthen the economic and social status of the common man. The DM serves the common man in every way. The DM lives among the public and improves their well-being by serving them.

Out of the PM, CM and DM, generally speaking people have maximum reach to the DM and therefore faith too. There is a belief among the public that if there is any problem, they can approach the DM and the solution will be found. The common citizen has the belief that the DM is the medicine for all ailments. There is also the fear that if they commit any mistake, then they will have to go to jail. DM is the biggest and most powerful post. That's why common people expect a lot from it and are also afraid of it. However, in recent years, the post of district magistrate has not fulfilled the expectations of the public. Hence, the attitude of the public has changed from positive to negative. Eliminating the negativity and regaining the lost faith is a big challenge for the IAS fraternity of the whole country. Accepting this challenge, during my first tenure of only one and a half years as DM, Banda, I brought laurels to the district in the state, country and abroad by introducing more than 20 innovations through public participation, through the system and resources available in the district. These innovations increased the water level by 1.34 metres, made the jail rank number one in the state through prison reforms and increased the crop productivity by more than 18.5 per cent. People-participatory model was created for 'reducing malnutrition'. By altering the direction and condition of the students, they were made to tread the right path. The farmer's awareness was increased which made them move towards increasing their income. The capability and income of women was increased by bringing them to the forefront.

I went to Banda for the first time on 31 August 2018 and reached there at 6 p.m. where I was handed over the charge as District Magistrate, Banda in the Treasury by Shri Vinod Kumar, Chief Treasury Officer. Many thoughts were running through my mind on way to Banda. This post challenged me to think whether or not I would be able to do justice to this post as expected.

I had become DM for the first time. I used to ask myself—will I be able to run the affairs of the district? I felt that the post of District Magistrate was very big. I had doubts in my mind. I kept getting distracted. There was turmoil going on in my mind. I had more than 24 years of experience in various positions including Deputy Collector, Additional District Magistrate and Chief Development Officer but still there was a lot of confusion in my mind and there was a big challenge of running the district.

According to the report of the Institute of Applied Statistics and Development Studies, 2016, Banda has some significant challenges like:

- Poor agriculture
- Limited access to technical knowledge
- Non-availability of irrigation water
- Fallow land
- Poor infrastructure
- Poor health facilities
- Improper public distribution system
- Inefficient execution of government schemes
- Migration and unemployment
- Malnutrition status

Banda is a district in the state of Uttar Pradesh with a population of 1.8 million. Banda is an underdeveloped and backward district of the Bundelkhand region of Uttar Pradesh. The entire area of the district was suffering from water scarcity. According to the study, 71 per cent of the wells were in dire condition. The main economic activity here is agriculture. Agriculture was a loss-making business. That is why most of the people drifted away from agriculture and no one wanted to take up agriculture work voluntarily. Those who had no alternative were engaged in agriculture and were leading a life of poverty and deprivation. Most people had a sense of despair that nothing can happen here. No development can take place with a defeated mindset. There was a great void between the public and the district administration. The image of the administration was not good among the general public and there was a lack of credibility. Most of the people did not even have money in their bank account. They had only a little capital of water, forest and land. With this capital, I started an effort to bring development, greenery and happiness to their lives. From time to time and continuously, we undertook one task after another. Disappointment started fading away and hope began to grow.

25 जनवरी 2019

बांदा जागरण

डीएम की पहल से सड़कों पर घटे अन्ना पशु, सरकारी आवास में मॉडल कृषि फार्म व आदर्श तालाब निर्माण

साझा किया सुख-दु:ख, सेतु बन निकाला हल

अन्ना पशु न छोड़ने पर आई जागरूकता

किसानों की पाठशाला, जल संरक्षण का संदेश

ये हैं उपलब्धियां

प्रतिभा को बेहतर मंच देने के प्रयास

अनूठी पहल : इनोवेशन स्टार्टअप समिट

We started with complex water problem-solving. More than 20 successful innovations were implemented one after the other during one and a half years. Participation of the people increased in finding innovative solutions to all problems through contact, communication and cooperation.

It became a mass movement. Everyone was inspired and participated voluntarily and contributed greatly. Good governance increased through dialogue. Expected results were also obtained. To achieve something good, you must do something different. We adopted three new approaches to all programmes:

1. Work had to be done with the funds, resources, wealth, etc., available in the district. We would not ask for anything separately from outside.
2. Active participation of all concerned and relevant departments and stakeholders was obtained and all concerned people contributed by adopting the programme as their own.
3. We did low-cost or zero-cost work.

बाँदा जा

दैनिक जागरण

डीएम हीरा लाल के एक साल बेमिशाल

31 अगस्त 2018 को जनपद में किया था कार्यभार ग्रहण

पीएम ने डीएम की थी सराहना

- जिले का मतदान प्रतिशत बढ़ाकर देश भर में बटोरी सुर्खियाँ
- जल संरक्षण के अभियान से निकाली पानी संकट की तोड़
- अब कुपोषण मिटाने के लिये शुरू किया अभियान

जिलाधिकारी के चलाये गये अभियान

❑

3.1

Water Problem and Solution

In mid-September, 2018, I faced a law-and-order situation. An important road was blocked. SDM Banda Ms. Thameem Ansaria said that the reason for that was the failure of the water supply pump which had not been working for a week. This incident alerted me, and I began to collect information from people about the problem of water scarcity in the approaching summer months.

I did discussion with senior citizens, experts working in the water sector, veteran journalists and officials. Everyone shared how wells, ponds and rivers were the main sources of water 40 years ago, which people used for drinking water and irrigation. The changing lifestyle gradually separated the common man from natural sources and people started using tube wells and 'bottled water' (symbolically speaking). This situation of disconnection from water sources created the water crisis as people stopped taking care of natural water sources and started neglecting them. Gradually, these water sources were ruined and disappeared.

I was born and brought up in Bagdeeh, a remote backward village in Basti district of Uttar Pradesh. We had our own private well. It was the source of drinking water for us and our fellow villagers. We used to irrigate our crops with river water and pond water. My family and all the villagers used to take bath in the water of the pond in summer. This childhood experience of mine served as the basic knowledge to find a concrete solution for Banda.

When I went to Banda as DM for the first time, I already knew the problem of water scarcity. The problem of water scarcity was the biggest challenge for many people. Banda is infamous for its water crisis. I had been reading about water scarcity in Banda for a long time. I first went to Banda on 31 August 2018, as District Magistrate. The water problem was an issue about which I knew from day one as I had often read news about the water problem in Banda and watched the news about it on TV. The first problem of unrest that came up there in September was that of water. This problem made me alert and watchful. Upon enquiring, I came to know that there were daily demonstrations in summer. The women held demonstrations with water pots and presented bangles to the DM. This information cautioned me, "Start finding the solution right away, District Magistrate Heera Lal, otherwise you will have trouble during summer."

The people here used to fetch water from wells, ponds and rivers in the past. For the past many years, the changing lifestyle had made people turn away from these water sources. People started to use taps and tube wells. Drinking bottled water had become a symbol of pride and prestige. Due to this, people drifted away from the treasures of water (well, pond and river) and life-giving water sources were ignored. As a result, there was a severe day-to-day water crisis in the lives of the people. Happiness and greenery started decreasing in everyone's life. There was no drinking water or enough water for irrigation. Productivity declined and poverty increased. Many more problems have now arisen due to the scarcity of water, about which we are not even aware. Development was hindered. Shri Uma Shankar Pandey has done good work on water conservation in Jakhni village. Jakhni is known as Jal Gram.

On 6 October 2018, one-day 'Jal Sanrakshan Mahaparv' workshop was organised in the hall of Agricultural University. In the workshop basic information about saving and conserving water was given to the team of the village head, lekhpal and village secretary, and everyone was told that rainwater has to be conserved. This campaign started from this meeting. Water problem was made a public concern and issue. After this, in the first phase (from 7/12/2018) a mining drive was carried out around the wells and government taps. To begin with a team of junior engineers posted in the district was sent to Lucknow (11/01/2019) where they were given technical information and training by Shri Mahendra Modi, the then IPS. These same people passed the acquired technical knowledge to the workers in the village, and block so that quality work was done.

2,443 ponds were dug in 470 villages. A new place to collect 3,930 kilolitres of water was created. Around 34,732 people participated and became aware. Annual recharge capacity of 11,001 kilolitres was created.

For this work, the team was given an award by Shri Parameswaran Iyer, Secretary to the Government of India on 24 May 2019 in Delhi. This created excitement in the entire team. It also proved that we were making efforts in the right direction. I was not active yet. This was going on under the leadership of Shri Heera Lal, the then Chief Development Officer. The award woke me up. I became active. The second phase was started as soon as the May 2019 Lok Sabha elections were over. In this phase, the focus was on the wells and ponds. Around 7,800 wells were counted for the first time. A scheme was prepared to repair about 2,200 public and as many private ponds.

Phase-II began with the slogan 'We will bring water to the wells and ponds—we will make Banda happy'. The old attachment of the common man to the wells and ponds started getting established again. People started caring about them. They cleaned and maintained wells. The lack of knowledgeable people for cleaning wells became a hindrance as it was a risky task to enter the well. The excavation of the new pond was done by running a campaign under MGNREGA and Apna Khet Talab Yojana. This campaign was a unique experiment in India. The dependence of people on taps, tube wells and bottled water was reduced. For the first time, a campaign was launched to connect the common man with the home of water (habitat), i.e., wells, ponds, rivers. In my meetings, I used to say philosophically, "I want to dig a well, a pond, a river in the hearts, minds and thoughts of the people. It doesn't matter if the well is not dug on the ground on the spot, but the well must be dug in the hearts, minds and thoughts of the people." With this, a sense of respect, reverence, love and attachment for water sources was to be created in the mind of the common man. This slogan worked very well. The software of water (thought about water) was corrected with this statement.

If the software is correct, the hardware will automatically be fine and the entire water ecosystem will be fine.

This campaign was widely publicised and broadcast by newspapers, news portals, and TV. Due to this, the idea of saving water was created among the people associated with water and the public, i.e., the software was put in place.

देश में पहले नंबर पर पहुंचा तालाब कुआं जियाओ अभियान

जल संरक्षण

बांदा में जल संरक्षण के लिए लगातार प्रयास किए जा रहे हैं। जन भागेदारी भी इस अभियान में सुनिश्चित हो रही है। ऐसे में अभियान को धरातल पर ले जाने में आसानी होगी। इस अभियान को सही दिशा देना ही मेरा मुख्य उद्देश्य है।
हीरा लाल, जिलाधिकारी बांदा

- जल शक्ति मंत्रालय ने की अभियान की सराहना
- देश में चलाए गए छह अभियानों की हुई चर्चा
- उत्तर प्रदेश के तीन जिलों ने इसपर किया बेहतर काम

जागरण संवाददाता, बांदा : जल संरक्षण को लेकर चलाये जाने वाले अभियानों में बांदा का तालाब - कुंआ जियाओ अभियान की गूंज पूरे देश में पहुंच चुकी है। भारत सरकार के जल शक्ति मंत्रालय द्वारा जल संरक्षण के लिए शुरू किये गए अभियान में उत्तर प्रदेश के तीन जिलों के अभियानों को सर्वोच्च प्राथमिकता दी गई है। इसमें पहले स्थान पर बांदा का तालाब कुंआ अभियान दूसरे स्थान पर जालौन जिले का भूजल कोस संचय अभियान व तीसरे स्थान पर चित्रकूट जिले का मंदाकिनी नदी सफाई अभियान है। पूरे देश भर से चलाये जाने वाले अभियानों में छह अभियानों को प्राथमिकता दी गई है। जिनमें तीन उत्तर प्रदेश के हैं वहीं तीन अन्य में उत्तराखंड, केरल और झारखंड राज्य के चलाये गए जल संरक्षण अभियान हैं।

भारत सरकार के जल शक्ति मंत्रालय द्वारा गुरुवार को नई दिल्ली में जल संरक्षण अभियान की शुरुवात की गई। कार्यक्रम को विस्तार देने से पूर्व जल शक्ति मंत्रालय के सचिव यूपी सिंह ने देश भर में उत्कृष्ट रुप से जल संरक्षण अभियान चलाने वाले प्रदेशों की चर्चा की। इनमें सबसे बेहतर अभियान चलाने वाले प्रदेशों में उत्तर प्रदेश रहा। सचिव ने बताया कि उत्तर प्रदेश के तीन जिलों ने इस अभियान पर बेहतर काम शुरू किया है। इनमें बांदा अव्वल है। बांदा का तालाब- कुंआ जियाओ अभियान जनभागेदारी का रुप ले रहा है। गांव-गांव जलस्त्रोतों को लेकर आम लोगों में जागरुकता आ रही है। इसी प्रकार में जालौन का भूजल कोस अभियान और चित्रकूट का मंदाकिनी स्वच्छता अभियान भी बेहतर रुप ले रहा है।

सचिव ने तीनों जिलों की कार्ययोजना का सराहा है। पूरे देश में अभियान की सराहना होने एवं देश के जल शक्ति मंत्रालय द्वारा अपने एजेंडे में शामिल करने के बाद बांदा जिले की एक नई पहचान बनी है। जिलाधिकारी द्वारा चलाये इस अभियान पर स्थानीय तौर पर भी हर रोज सफलता की एक नई कड़ी जुड़ रही है।

The hearts and minds of the people were filled with thoughts of water. The misuse of water started decreasing. Common people started trying to save rainwater. Several programmes were organised to create this situation:

1. An inter-departmental committee was formed and I personally reviewed the weekly action plan.
2. Water budget was discussed in each of the 470 villages. Jal Choupal (a platform for water issues) was organised in every village. Due to this, the public was connected with the issue of water.
3. The first drive of pond digging was vigorous and successful.
4. Jal Aarti (worship of water) was started on three rivers of Banda—Ken, Baghein and Yamuna. An awareness campaign was conducted in 130 villages on the banks of the three rivers— 'Save the river, keep it clean, become rich from the river'.
5. Water march was taken out. Jal Aarti was performed at the water sources. On various occasions, 'Deep Dan' was organised on the water sources (well, pond, river).
6. 'Save trees' campaign and 'fencing' campaign were carried out.
7. Shri Raju Srivastava (comedian) was invited to the conference on poetry and music about water.

Shri U. P. Singh, Secretary, Ministry of Jal Shakti, Government of India came to know about Banda's unprecedented water conservation campaign from the media. In a telephonic discussion with him, I requested him to visit the spot and see the campaign. He made a two-day visit to Banda on 6 and 7 July 2020. He saw all kinds of tasks on the spot. He liked the work done regarding water conservation with public participation. He also gave a lot of publicity to the Banda model of water conservation so that others could adopt and take advantage of this model of public participation. Its main attraction was to work on wells, ponds, and rivers simultaneously in the entire district as a 50-year-old complex problem was being solved.

Shri U. P. Singh said that the rainy season was about to start and that the campaign would stop. We found an answer and on the suggestion of Ms. Prashansa Gupta, who was the district in-charge of the local NGO partner, rainwater harvesting facilities were created in 88 offices, 2,200 primary schools and unused wells. This campaign went on throughout the rainy season. After that, I started the weekly Aarti on the River. I also started monthly Aarti at Chilla, the confluence of Baghein and Yamuna. Some journalists said that the district magistrate was taking us back to the olden days of worship to distract and divert attention from the problem of water. I had to face this opposition, but my task was not to be religious but to connect the common man with all the sources of water and create awareness in them.

Mr Farooq, Mr Puneet and Mr Shishir of Water Aid, Lucknow gave all kinds of support as Knowledge Partners. The Country Head of Water Aid, Delhi, Mr M. K. Madhavan gave full support. At the local level, Ms. Prashansa Gupta continued to give impetus to the campaign. This experiment with PPP model was very successful.

Due to this work, in about one and a half years, the water level increased by about 1.34 metres. This in turn increased crop productivity by about 18.5 per cent. People themselves started saving water. Water became a part of people's thought process. People's love for water sources started increasing.

We have received many state and country level awards. This model was discussed all over the country.

एक अपील **|| पानी का पुण्य कमाओ ||**

"पुराने जमाने में खेत, तालाब से पानी पीता था। इंसान, कुएं से पानी पीता था। तालाब, तालाब नहीं रहा। कुएं और तालाब सूख गये। जब से कुएं-तालाबों ने हमारा साथ छोडा, तब से पानी का विकट संकट हमारे सामने आ गया है। वर्तमान जीवन और भविष्य को यदि सुरक्षित करना है तो तालाब और कुएं को पुनः जीवित कर, दोस्त एवं जीवन साथी बनाना होगा। तालाब और कुएं हमारे लिए पूज्यनीय है। पुनः हमें इनकी पूजा शुरू कर देनी चाहिए। यह हमारी बाध्यता है- इस सच्चाई को समझना होगा। सामूहिक श्रमदान और आपसी सहयोग (पुरानी रीति-रिवाज) से तालाब-कुओं को पुनजीवित करना होगा। यदि ऐसा नहीं किया तो क्या होगा ? भीषण गर्मी एवं गम्भीर जल संकट इसके भयावह परिणाम के संकेत दे रहे हैं।"

जल ही जीवन है
जल है तो कल है

हीरा लाल I.A.S.
जिलाधिकारी, बाँदा

पानी बड़ा सवाल था बाँदा की जमीं पर।
जीना बड़ा मुहाल था बाँदा की जमीं पर।
मैंने फिर इस सवाल को शर्मिन्दा कर दिया।
सूखे कुएँ तालाब को फिर जिंदा कर दिया।

—नज़रे आलम 'नज़र बाँदवी'

❑

3.2

Start-up and Innovation

Be the change you want to see in the world.

—Mahatma Gandhi

28–30 January 2018

According to a report by the United Nations Development Programme and NITI Aayog, Banda was lagging behind in several development indicators, such as, Banda's per capita income is only 43 per cent of India's average. Similarly, indicators such as production per worker and production per hectare of agriculture (net sown area), the condition of Banda was poor. Overall, Banda was ranked sixth in the Bundelkhand region, which was disappointing. Most of the people had a sense of despair, a feeling like that of a defeated soldier. They felt that Banda was backward and could never progress. Most of the people seemed to have lost their hope and courage. They were desperate and disillusioned and had left everything to God. A three-day innovative event was organised to change this mindset.

Its purpose was to find and adopt a simple, easy and low-cost permanent solution to the problem of the food system, malnutrition, water crisis, unemployment and poverty. The aim was to create the thought process of innovation in the mind and intellect so that people could think scientifically and positively and move forward with strength and courage.

District Science Club Co-coordinator, Shri Shani Kumar laid the foundation of this program. He had done good work through the club. The preparation was started based on his experience. During the preparation, we realized that this task was quite complicated and troublesome. After preparing for a few days, we realized that we would have many sleepless nights. We decided not to go ahead with it. After a month, suddenly a thought came to my mind that we should do it, only then would we get the solution for the problem. I gathered courage and fixed the dates of the program from January 28 to 30, 2019 and started preparing vigorously. I contacted Mr. Arpit Gupta, event manager of Elets, a past acquaintance. Mr. Arpit Gupta is a resident of Banda. We made Elets, the Knowledge Partner. Mr. Arpit Gupta gave us full support. The officials of the Science and Technology Council, Uttar Pradesh, Lucknow participated in the program and played an important role in completing it after making full preparations. Mr Sandeep Dwivedi and Mr. Radhelal remained on the spot and gave us the full support of their experience of conducting the innovation workshop. But the then principal secretary and director did not extend the expected cooperation.

In common parlance, it can be said that every start-up innovation is a bundle of knowledge. In this, there is a thought of taking risks and doing something new. In this summit, many start-up innovations were introduced among the assemblage of intellectuals. The main objective behind this event was that the people of the district should become acquainted with start-up and innovation so that they could get attached to these two words and could reach their desired destination easily and without difficulty, along with finding solutions to their problems. A new vision of change can be created in each person.

No such event had taken place in the district in the past. So, there was a wave of joy and enthusiasm among the people. It proved that the people here were willing to acquire and adopt knowledge and innovation. In this arrangement, along with the officers of the district administration, participation was also garnered from the public, journalists, businessmen and many organizations who fully cooperated in organizing this mega event.

Key issues/themes of the Summit

Innovation and start-ups for sustainable development

Sub-theme

- Rural and urban development
- From agriculture to agribusiness
- Medicine, health and hygiene
- Education, educational process and educational environment
- Technology for social development
- Water conservation and management
- Changes over time in traditional, social, cultural heritage

During the discussion at the summit, the residents of district Banda were divided into five classes:

1. Students
2. Trained people
3. Untrained masses
4. Farmers
5. Trained public (the subject of training can be anything. It means that the participant is trained in some subject, i.e., possesses formal qualification)

Stages of activities at the Innovation and Start-up Summit 2019:

1. Inauguration and closing ceremony of Innovation and Start-up Summit 2019
2. Conducting technical sessions
3. Stalls and exhibitions of various departments
4. Cultural program

Twenty-eight sessions were organized in the workshop on the issues of various local problems. A lot of necessary informations were given to the public by setting up 80 government and non-government exhibitions/stalls. It was attended by 135 innovators from across the country.

This successful event became a unique example for the Bundelkhand region. The following were the benefits of this three-day event:

1. The district got a new identity and its image improved.
2. Everyone's mindset changed. Everyone's sense of despair turned into hope. The thought of change arose in the government employees that anything could be done in a backward district like Banda. Everyone became optimistic.
3. People were introduced to low-cost, simple solutions to problems.
4. Everyone got an opportunity/platform to show their talent and aptitude. This energized the people.
5. The gap between the government and the people was reduced, which increased mutual coordination and harmony. The idea of achieving good governance was formed.
6. Everyone's self-confidence and assurance increased.
7. The entire district came on one platform, due to which everyone realized the power of Banda.

With this event, the whole district came on one platform and started in a positive direction on a new path. Most people thought that something good had to be done and changes made. The best change was reflected in the hearts, minds and thinking of the officers/employees. This ceremony pushed the blocked mindset of development and made it run. The belief that good and positive development can take place in Banda also awakened in everyone's mind. Due to this thinking, many innovative programs

and projects were done one after the other and all received expected success. Everyone was happy due to continuous programs. Gradually, everyone became energetic and the caravan continued to grow. The work culture changed and everyone started enjoying working in the new positive environment. The power of love and affection changed the atmosphere. There was a rise in mutual relations, coordination, contact, dialogue and cooperation among the general public. For the first time, entire Banda came on one platform and agreed on the issue of development that Banda had to be changed. Everyone also realized the power of Banda. The caravan was formed and the journey began. It was the most exciting and thrilling program of the last several decades. This became an example for entire Bundelkhand. It was discussed positively at the state and country level.

It was a beginning that proved to be a 'milestone'. It filled the common man with zeal to move forward. The result was that people automatically started moving forward with positive thinking and started doing something new. A small change is part of a big success.

मुद्दत से बेबसी के जो मारे हुए थे हम।
जीवन की हर लड़ाई को हारे हुए थे हम।
स्टार्टअप का डी.एम. ने दीपक जला दिया।
मायूसियों का दिल से अँधेरा मिटा दिया।

—नज़रे आलम 'नज़र बाँदवी'

नई-नई तकनीक को अपनाकर खुशहाली के रास्ते बढ़ेंगे बुंदेली, समस्याओं का त्वरित हल निकालने में मील का पत्थर साबित होगा यह आयोजन

स्टार्टअप समिट से अब फैलेगा रोजगार का उजियारा

कई स्टालों में दी जा रही योजनाओं की जानकारी

नवाचार के जरिए जिले को देश भर में मिली शोहरत

उम्मीद-2020

3.3

Lok Sabha Elections—2019

(A festival of strengthening democracy)

The most important basis for a good election is a good electoral roll. The Election Commission of India, by running a special campaign from 1 to 30 September 2018, got the voter list updated and corrected as per the instructions of the Commission. 38,831 new voters were added. Other parameters of the commission were also improved. In this project, I worked as District Election Officer. It was headed by Sub-district Election Officer, Shri Santosh Bahadur Singh, Additional District Officer, Finance and Revenue. On 25 January 2019, on National Voters' Day, 6 districts of the state received awards for doing good work in the rolls. Banda was also included in it. The Governor, Chief Secretary presented these awards in Lucknow.

राष्ट्रीय मतदाता दिवस

25 जनवरी, 2019

प्रशस्ति-पत्र

श्री हीरा लाल,

This created enthusiasm among all the concerned personnel. After this, the Innovation and Start-up Summit held on January 28, 29 and 30, 2019 created a wave of new ideas in the entire district. The unprecedented success of the two programs and the pressure of preparations for the election in May 2019 came in handy. The next campaign would be elections. We decided to do something good and different in the election and started brainstorming about it.

The commission had three main goals:

1. Good electoral roll,
2. Higher voting percentage, and
3. To conduct the voting peacefully in a festive atmosphere.

मजबूत लोकतंत्र की बुनियाद करेंगे।
इतिहास वो रचेंगे कि सब याद करेंगे।
मतदान होगा नब्बे प्लस अब चुनाव में।
सरकार हम बनाएँगे शहरों में, गाँव में।

—नज़रे आलम 'नज़र बाँदवी'

We had won in the electoral roll. The name of Banda district also appeared among the 6 best districts out of 75 districts. The first step was successful. The next goal was how to increase the turnout.

In order to understand the election, old data was perused by the Election Office. India's polling average in the 2014 Lok Sabha elections was 66.38 per cent, that of UP was 58.29 per cent and that of Banda was 52.69 per cent. The voting percentage of Banda was much less than both the country and the state. The average turnout in the 2017 assembly elections was 60.20 per cent. This also proves that the voting in the 2014 Lok Sabha election was less than that of Vidhan Sabha. In the 2015 Panchayat elections, in two-gram panchayats, i.e., in Kolaval Raipur (Mahua block) 91.98 per cent voting was recorded and in Shahpatan (Naraini block) 90.7 per cent voting was recorded.

Analysis of the data showed that more than 90 per cent of the voting took place in two booths. If there could be more than 90 per cent voting in the panchayat, then why not in the Lok Sabha? We took it as a challenge and started working seriously.

We set a target that 13,09,009 voters of Banda had to cast more than 90 per cent of votes in 1,454 booths at 843 polling stations. The campaign was launched—

With 90%+ voter turnout—Banda to become the pride of the country

A simple, easy and robust strategy was created to achieve this impossible goal. Public participation was made its mainstay.

Association for Democratic Reforms (ADR) is a non-governmental organisation. It is doing great work for electoral reforms. It was made Knowledge Partner. Its state coordinator was Mr Anil Sharma. We held meetings for public awareness in the four assemblies with the help of ADR and motivated everyone to actively participate in the election process.

New steps towards new goals:

- Use of cultural programmes.
- Appointed three new election brand ambassadors.
- Appointed 2,916 booth ambassadors.
- Internship for school children in a format and certificates were given.
- Twenty-thousand letters were written for voting.
- Transport facility was provided.
- Efforts were made to call voters residing outside the district.
- Participation of NCC/Scouts/Rovers/Rangers in the voting.
- Voting fair.
- Linking various government and non-government organisations.
- Each worker's own booth (by 8,161 officers/staff members).

- Special facility to 9,154 Divyang voters (differently abled voters).
- Knowledge partner team.
- War Room.
- Advisory Board.
- New methods of promotion and publicity.
- Best voting reward.
- Way to reach each voter—by SOP.
- Women motivational committees.
- Intensive monitoring.
- Media management.
- Motivational slogan.
- Additional use of election help number—1950.

On 28 February 2019, the commission took a review in the Tilak Hall of Lucknow Legislative Assembly—

A review meeting regarding the preparation for the Lok Sabha elections—2019 was organized by the Election Commission of India, New Delhi by the office of the Chief Electoral Officer, Lucknow. In this meeting, all the high officials, Commissioners, District Magistrates, Superintendent of Police, and all the officers and employees of the Election Commission connected with the state elections were present. Chief Commissioner Shri Sunil Arora and both the Election Commissioners Shri Ashok Lavasa and Shri Sushil Chandra were also present. When the Election Commission asked for details of the activities towards increasing the voting percentage in Banda, I apprised them of all the aspects of the 90 per cent action plan. I also presented a copy of the promotional material like the handbill, pad, banner, etc.

In view of the hot weather during the elections, the information about the arrangement for drinking water was taken by the Election Commission. On February 28, the ambitious plan of 90 per cent came to the notice of the entire commission and all the officers of Uttar Pradesh. Learning about the action plan of 90 per cent in the meeting, the officials also felt awkward because prima facie increasing the target to 90 per cent voting from 52.69 per cent (2014) was like a dream.

Shri Umesh Sinha, deputy election commissioner, Election Commission of India, New Delhi reviewed the election preparation at Yojna Bhawan, Lucknow on 2nd March 2019. Systematic Voters Education and Electoral Participation (SVEEP) is a scheme run by the Election Commission of India. It aims at an overall increase in the percentage of voting at polling stations during the current electoral process as compared to the previous Assembly and Parliamentary elections. At the same time, conducting inclusive elections with the active participation of excluded communities, bridging the gender gap and increasing awareness about EVMs and VVPATs are also important objectives of this scheme. In this meeting, only two District Magistrates—me from Banda and Shri Kaushal Raj Sharma, District Magistrate, Lucknow participated. I presented the action plan of Banda's ambitious 90 per cent voter turnout target.

3rd March 2019

A meeting was organised by ADR at Pt Deendayal Upadhyay State Institute of Rural Development, Lucknow. I participated in the technical session—'Role of Youth & Voter Awareness: In Preparation for General Election' of the 15th Annual National Conference on Electoral and Political Reforms. I presented the action plan to achieve the target of 90 per cent voter turnout very effectively. Everyone appreciated—the way of presentation and the goal. The Chief Electoral Officer of the state, Mr L. Venkateswaralu spoke about extending all kinds of cooperation to achieve this goal. The campaign was based on increasing the awareness and participation of youth in the Lok Sabha elections—2019.

Meeting of Additional Chief Secretary, Information

14th March 2019—Collectorate Auditorium, Banda.

Additional Chief Secretary, Information, Shri Awanish Awasthi participated in the meeting of gram panchayat secretaries in the Collectorate Auditorium. He appreciated the effective efforts being made by the district administration for more than 90 per cent voting. He called making the differently abled voters awareness and arranging RAM/vehicle facilities in the polling stations for them and their participation in cultural programs, and the formation of women committees to motivate female voters, a good step. He praised the arrangement of polling fairs at 843 centres in the district.

Financial assistance was provided by the Information Department for the campaign and publicity for voters under the guidelines of SVEEP. Shri K K Pandey, Deputy Commissioner NRLM, Shri Bhupendra Singh Yadav, Deputy Director, Information, Shri Hira Lal, retired Chief Development Officer, Ms Sharda, Additional District Information Officer, Shri Angad Prasad Sharma and officers from various departments were present in the meeting.

Prime Minister Shri Narendra Modi's (25/04/2019) public meeting at Banda University of Agriculture and Technology, Banda:

The Prime Minister of India, Shri Narendra Modi, praised the campaign being run by Dr. Heera Lal, District Magistrate, Banda and his team for 90 per cent voter turnout at the Vijay Sankalp rally in Banda. He said in his address, "There is election machinery in elections. It keeps telling us to do this, not to do that, etc., in elections. I was told that the election officers of this district are working hard for 100 per cent voting, this is a very good thing. I congratulate them and I will also tell the Election Commission that what I have heard, if it is true, is how they are creating public awareness, making voters aware of the Election

Commission, talking about democracy beyond politics. So, the Election Commission of India should also look towards such hard-working officers all over the country, if not in this election, then in the coming elections, regarding what methods they adopt, how they mobilise people. They must document all such things. I congratulate… what I heard..."

Prime Minister Shri Narendra Modi also recommended to the Election Commission of India that the work of officers undertaking the task of public awareness in this way and giving importance to their campaign should be followed across the country in the upcoming elections.

Historic achievements of the campaign

Lok Sabha elections—2019, turned out to be a golden memory for Banda. Earlier, there used to be noise or ruckus in the elections; this time it did not happen. We launched a campaign to change the target of 85 per cent given by the Election Commission to 90 per cent. The voting percentage is a measure of the strength of a democracy. The higher the voting percentage, the stronger the country and democracy will be restored. The District Magistrate also explained that it was the biggest and best opportunity to serve the country. Common people were inspired to serve the country and they associated themselves with this campaign. Gradually, this caravan kept on increasing, due to which its voice resonated not only in the state but in the country. That is why Hon'ble Prime Minister Shri Narendra Modi mentioned it in his speech. Inspired by the thoughts of the District Magistrate, this goal gradually became a mass movement. This campaign created a new history. It showed every person the way to do something new in life. Some of the achievements of this campaign were as follows:

- After a long time, the whole district came together agreeing on one issue. People's support was received, due to which a sense of unity and cooperation was created in the district. The habit of hard work and positive thinking developed in people. Everyone joined the campaign voluntarily without any pressure to gain joy.

- The enthusiasm of the voters in the scorching heat at the time of elections was worth seeing.
- Due to the scheme to felicitate the first voter at each booth, there was a race to vote at the booth since morning. All the 1,454 first voters were felicitated and given a citation.
- During the entire campaign, there was a celebration of cultural programs. The cultural platform made voters aware through local artists in the villages and city. The new artists of the district got a platform to perform their talent. The cultural heritage of Banda had a chance to come into the limelight.
- In this mass movement, the campaign was given momentum through the appointment of three young, talented and energetic girl students as brand ambassadors. Due to this, they received recognition and fame in the district. Apart from this, children got an opportunity to showcase their talent through cultural programs at each booth.
- Youth who became voters for the first time were appointed booth ambassadors. With this, they became aware of their important role and responsibilities in democracy at a young age. While working at the booth, they became an important link between the village and the booth.
- There was an opportunity to teach school and college students about democracy along with their studies. The students studying in the training institutes, along with their studies learnt practical measures to strengthen democracy through internships.
- The DM sent a letter with his signature to more than 20,000 people inviting them to join him in this campaign. This increased the engagement and attraction of the people to the district administration. The distance between the District Magistrate and the public was reduced.

- The DM's handbill created storm during the entire campaign. Wherever he went for the program, he had the handbill *'DM ka patrak aaya hai, voting ka sandesha laya hai'* distributed to the audience. Due to this, every reader and listener connected with this campaign. They called it DM's invitation, due to which people of every section started feeling connected with this mass movement.
- Use of various means of publicity, such as banners, stickers on vehicles, letters, LED vans, displays, social networking sites, YouTube, Facebook, WhatsApp, carry bags, scarves, etc., to motivate and inspire the public in the campaign led to a spark in voting; when these means passed before the voters many times; they were inspired to vote. A T-shirt and cap with the target became a status symbol during the campaign. Those wearing the T-shirt and a cap with the target automatically became disseminators of the message. This outfit with inspiring print impressed the voters.

- In previous elections, vehicles were not allowed up to the booth. This time the voter was allowed to take their vehicle upto 200 metres from the booth. With the permission for the vehicle, the old, handicapped and unwell voters could easily reach the booth for voting. This decision greatly increased the enthusiasm of the voters.
- Efforts were made to contact and call the family, friends and neighbours of voters living outside the district. Handbills and video clips were sent to them through WhatsApp. In the adjoining border districts, Deputy Labour Commissioner Shri Anurag Mishra was sent as a representative of the District Magistrate, Banda. He appealed to the high officials of the Labour Departments, labour contractors to send the labourers of Banda living in their area.
- Letters were sent to the District Magistrates of other districts, urging them to send the labourers of Banda viz, Fatehpur, Rae-bareily, rural Kanpur, Prayagraj districts.
- Efforts were also made to contact and call the voters living outside using the helpline of the Election Commission—1950.
- For successful participation of women, district level, block level, village level and booth level trained teams were formed under Women Awareness Committee. These women motivational committees did the work of encouraging half the population to come out of the house. Due to this, women empowerment was experienced by everyone.
- Women actively participated in this and understood the importance of themselves in democracy and explained it to the people.
- To achieve the goal, discussions were held with each section of the society (village watchmen, daily wage workers, sweepers, retired teachers, etc.). Due to this, the gap between them and

the bureaucratic class was erased and every class realized that they are a very important and integral part of society.

- Wheelchairs were arranged for differently abled people for voting. They were also given special attention at the booth. They realized their importance in society and their inferiority complex decreased. Out of a total of 9,154 Divyang voters, 7,813 voted. Their voter turnout was 85.35 per cent. Dr. Preeti, district disabled officer did a great job in this.

- The campaign led to new job opportunities for people running printing presses and such small ventures throughout the city.
- In this election, each officer/employee adopted one booth (total of 8,161) and went to the voters and connected with the people. The DM himself set the model by adopting a booth himself. He listened to everyone's problems. This not only gave momentum and energy to 90+ per cent campaign but also removed negative thoughts from the minds of the people.
- The campaign brought people from government and non-government organizations closer. The DM had meetings with

village development officers, accountants, traders, trade union, industrial board, BLOs, supervisors, pensioners, principals of colleges, ration distributors, PRDs, village heads, religious leaders, postmen, media personnel, bank workers, farmers, advocates, home guards, village employment workers, meter readers, chemists, sweepers, labourers, contractors, in-charges of NCC, NSS, and eunuchs and inspired all of them to contribute in this campaign. This led to the establishment of social coordination.

- During this, departmental and school rallies were started all over Banda. These rallies provided a considerable impetus to the campaign of 90+ per cent. These rallies led to public awareness and vigilance. Along with this, people were made aware through street plays and rangoli by children.
- Inspirational slogans related to the 90+ per cent campaign like *'Abki Baar, 90 Paar'*, *'90 pratishat ho matdaan, Banda bane desh ki shaan'*, *'90 pratishat matdaan karna hai, Banda ko bhavya banana hai'*, *'Banda naye lakshya ki ore'*, *'90 pratishat matdaan ka macha hai shor'*, etc., created a buzz and infused new energy and enthusiasm among the people. This woke everyone up.
- With the inspiration of the DM, not only government departments but also non-governmental organisations took out rallies. They held meetings at intersections and tried to make voters aware by taking out rallies with banners, flex etc. This was the first time that government, non-government and educational organisations together supported the DM, making 90+ per cent campaign their goal considering it their own.
- Women's war room was established to increase the active role of women. Through the war room, the work of monitoring and recording all the activities being conducted by women in the district was done due to which 90 per cent of the campaign achieved new heights.

Women motivational committees

Eight development block level, 471 village level and 1,454 booth level trained women committees were formed to bring half the population of the district (total number of women voters 5,93,689) to the polling booth. These committees enthused women voters and encouraged them to vote.

- Deputy Commissioner of National Rural Livelihoods Mission was made the nodal in-charge of the trained teams. The teams formed at the district level were divided into two parts. Ms. Shalini Jain of State Rural Livelihood Mission was made in-charge of the team constituted for rural area and the block development officer was made in-charge of urban area.

- Women associated with National Rural Livelihoods Mission played an important role in achieving the 90 per cent target.
- Twenty thousand active women of 2000 (two thousand) self-help groups in 8 development blocks of the district took the responsibility of their booths.

- Meeting was organized under women voter awareness team in every booth in every village a day before polling.
- On the day of polling, through the team *'Jagao Aur Bulao'*, women went door-to-door to bring women to the polling station and drop them home after voting.
- To increase the number of women voters, one pink booth was set up in each of the four assemblies, in which all the polling personnel were women.
- An intensive monitoring team was formed for this entire campaign. The team reviewed the entire campaign by monitoring it at the village and district levels. Its daily progress review was carried out by the DM. Any shortcomings found from time to time were rectified.
- This time each polling station (843) was decorated in a new way based on the concept of Gharati-Janavasa-Barati, with the provision of tents, chairs, rugs and cultural program with small refreshments. It attracted the voters. This was an important reason behind the increased voting percentage. This created enthusiasm among the voters.
- Through the campaign, students of NCC, NSS, Rovers and Rangers got the opportunity and experience to contribute on the day of the polling fair under community work and to do social service along with learning valuable lessons on democracy.
- Under the Best Voting Reward Scheme to motivate all the villages, the villages which had the highest voting percentage in the panchayat election—2015 were given solar lights as a reward. This encouraged the voters.
- Every gram panchayat BLO or everyone who performed well at the booth level was honoured with a citation. This motivated all the village BLOs to do good work so that their village could be recognized and they could also get the benefit of the government grant scheme.

- There was very good coordination between the police and the administration during this election. Good strategy and action plan were implemented together by the administration and the police, which led to a fair, peaceful and enthusiastic election.
- During the campaign, the Department of Information and Media (Print and Electronic) played an important role. They took every small and big news related to this campaign to the people. This goal was imprinted in the minds of people as they saw it many times, which inspired them to vote.
- During the campaign, government machinery reached villages. The officers met people in the villages, communicated with them and they understood their thoughts. This reduced the distance between the administration and the people, giving a thrust to good governance.
- Everyone who did excellent work in the campaign was honoured with a citation. This boosted the morale of those who did good work.
- The polling percentage of Lok Sabha elections—2019 is the highest ever polling percentage in Banda.
- The polling percentage of Banda was 52.69 per cent in Lok Sabha elections—2014, which increased to 63.24 per cent in Lok Sabha elections—2019. There was an increase of 10.55 per cent in the Lok Sabha elections—2019. Banda district occupies first place in the state in terms of percentage growth.
- In the Lok Sabha elections—2014, none of the booths in Banda had 90 per cent. In 2019, 7 booths crossed the magic figure of 90 per cent. That is a matter of pride.
- In the Lok Sabha elections—2019, there were 645 booths with more than 60 per cent and less than 70 per cent, 281 with more than 70 per cent and less than 80 per cent, 43 booths with more than 80 per cent and less than 90 per cent. This is also a historic achievement.

- The main message of this campaign for the people of the district was also to 'Make 90 per cent a part of your life, learn from it. Try to stay 90 plus in every aspect of life.' This feeling had developed. It proved helpful in making people's life happy.
- More than 25 per cent of voters live outside the district. Invitations were sent to them through homes, BLOs, booth adopters, 1950 helpline and other means. Leaflets and video clips were also sent to them. Those voters wondered about what was happening in this election. Even though they may not have cast their vote, they were kept abreast of the election activities.
- It developed team spirit among the people. People got a chance to learn the art of moving ahead by setting goals in life.

90 प्लस मतदान अभियान ने हीरालाल को बनाया 'हीरो'

पीएम मोदी ने मंच से की थी सराहना, निर्वाचन आयोग डीएम को दे रहा अवार्ड

डीएम हीरालाल।

लोकसभा चुनाव : बांदा के सात बूथ बने 90 प्लस के हीरो

दुरेड़ी में सबसे ज्यादा 96.6 व 94.25 फीसद वोटिंग से हटेटी पुरवा दूसरा स्थान पर

ये बूथ रहे मतदान में अव्वल

चुनाव प्रेक्षक व डीएम ने किया मंथन

This campaign helped the District Administration connect door-to-door, village-to-village, at street and settlement level and with the public. This will go a long way in promoting good governance. This instilled a belief in the people that when democracy is strong then our country, state and district will be strong. Keeping all these things in mind, this whole campaign got a new dimension. I was considered the inspiration for this. It was a miracle resulting from the hard work, dedication and passion of the entire team that this time there was a historic increase in voting percentage in every booth of the district. All these strategies will act as inspiration in future elections.

Again, on 25 December 2020, the Governor and Chief Secretary presented the award. The prime minister praised the election work of Banda alone out of 739 districts across the country. This is important and a matter of pride.

"No voter was left behind. In the Lok Sabha—2019 elections, DEO/DM Heera Lal worked at the grassroots level. In the public meeting held in Banda on 25 April 2019, even our Prime Minister appreciated his efforts. He has increased the voting percentage to the highest than ever before, he has created a model of election in the entire state, which is worthy of emulation in the upcoming elections for fundamentally strengthening democracy and quality participation."

—Shri L Venkateswaralu
The Then Chief Electoral Officer, Uttar Pradesh

'90 Per Cent Plus Initiative to Increase Voting Percentage during 2019 Lok Sabha elections'

"The vision of Dr. Heera Lal (former DM, Banda) was a unique and significant achievement in the electoral field. If the Banda model is replicated across the country, other districts have the potential to carry forward the SVEEP mandate of the Election Commission of India."

—Mr Rahul Verma
Fellow CPR, New Delhi

क्र. सं.	विधानसभा का नाम एवं मतदान दिवस	दिव्यागों की संख्या	मतदान करनेवाले दिव्यागों की कुल संख्या	मतदान प्रतिशत
1.	Tindwari	2193	1976	90.10
	(29.04.19)			
2.	Baberu			
	(06.05.19)	2557	2073	81.07
3.	Naraini			
	(06.05.19)	2622	2240	85.43
4.	Banda			
	(06.05.19)	1782	1524	85.50

❑

3.4

Freedom from the Curse of Malnutrition

When I was going to Banda to take charge as district magistrate, Banda, on my way, I received a call on my mobile from former acquaintance Ms Shailavi Sharda (Journalist for Times of India). Ms Shailavi said that she wanted to tell me about a unique thing. She told me that the people of Banda were not aware that Banda was a victim of malnutrition. She also told me that UNICEF had done a pilot project in Naraini block and that Ms Sharda had written the news about its success. After talking to her, I asked her for the newspaper clippings.

After reaching Banda, I enquired and learnt that the common man was not aware of the problem of malnutrition. Ms Sharda was right. The first and biggest challenge was how to make the public aware of the curse of malnutrition.

11,985 कुपोषित, 6649 बच्चों को सूखा रोग

यूनिसेफ की टीम ने कुपोषण का लिया जायजा, आंगनबाड़ी केंद्रों का किया निरीक्षण

बांदा का सुपोषण अभियान बन सकता है मॉडल

I collected complete information about the work in Naraini from UNICEF's Divisional Advisor, Ms Garima Singh. I directed to make a detailed action plan to implement the pilot results of Naraini block in all the 8 blocks of the district. The action plan was prepared with the help of UNICEF and others. For about four months, I made people aware by giving speeches on malnutrition at every meeting. Newspapers published it. Slowly it started to become an issue. It took about 6 months for people to become aware of it. Malnutrition became an issue. People started thinking of ways to avoid malnutrition. An action plan was also prepared to prevent it. For this money, resources, and necessary knowledge were arranged.

What is malnutrition?

First, I understood it in the rural language and then explained it to the people. Malnutrition is the lack of nutrients in the body, i.e., lack of proper nutrition.

There are 3 symptoms of malnutrition:

1. Less weight as per age.
2. Less height as per age.
3. Less weight as per height.

According to the National Family Health Survey (NFHS-4), malnutrition in Banda was 47 per cent and SAM (severe acute malnutrition) was 6.7 per cent.

UNICEF did a pilot project for children in Naraini block from December 2017 to November 2018. Under this, 57 out of 150 children got health benefits. This unique experiment says a lot and can have far-reaching consequences. Based on this, I started the Banda nutrition program. I formed a task force under the chairmanship of the District Magistrate. A plan was prepared to work with coordination between mining, health, women and child development, MGNREGA, Panchayati Raj, National Rural Livelihood Mission, and food and logistics department. Everyone participated with the available knowledge, money, resources, etc., in their department. NGOs like UNICEF were added. Special attention was given to the capacity-building of Anganwadi, ANM, and Asha Bahus. They were trained several times with the help of UNICEF and the necessary capacity-building was done.

First initiative: To get rid the malnourished from malnutrition.

Second initiative: Action plan to prevent malnutrition.

Only 1,69,199 children were registered in Anganwadi. According to the Health Department, 2,60,314 children were up to 5 years of age. Out of them, 1,27,930 (49 per cent) children were tested. A total of 6,649 (5.7 per cent) children were found to be acutely malnourished. 2,840 (2.4 per cent) children were found SAM. 11,985 (9.4 per cent) children were found to be underweight.

A campaign was launched to bring them out of malnutrition. 25 per cent of acutely malnourished, 17.1 per cent of SAM and

14.2 per cent of underweight children were cured of malnutrition. This historic result boosted everyone's morale. UNICEF and Banda signed a Memorandum of Understanding on 19 July 2019. It included 43 activities in 14 focus areas of 6 sectors. Every month, a UNICEF team from Lucknow came to Banda. One day was dedicated to a thorough review and advanced action plan. In this, problems were solved and further strategies were made.

We implemented it in a mission mode. Many other people and organisations working in this field became partners in this. Coordination, capacity-building and regular monitoring led us to the encouraging results, which continued to motivate and drive the team ahead.

A one-day workshop was organised on 24 August 2019 at Marriott Hotel, Lucknow. Its entire action plan was prepared under the leadership of Prof. Debashish Dasgupta, IIM Lucknow. Prof. Gupta addressed the workshop. It was led by Ms Ruth Liano, UNICEF, Uttar Pradesh, where all her advisers participated. Ten good performing personnel from each department of Banda district also participated. The purpose of this programme was to reflect on the results achieved till that time, to contemplate, to enhance the capacity, knowledge and enthusiasm of the people. We also considered how to implement this model in the entire state. UNICEF also started implementing this model in some aspirational districts.

NITI Aayog mentioned this model of Banda on page no. 73 in the progress report of *'Sahi Poshan, Desh Roshan'* campaign in September 2019. The biggest strength of this model was that it is community-based and the capacity-building of all the people associated with it has been done in all aspects related to fighting every type of malnutrition. For this, there was no additional demand for money from the state govt. and the work was done with the resources available in the district. The good results attained from the programme attracted everyone towards it. This is the reason that it was implemented even at the state level in many districts through UNICEF.

Main problem: The common man was not aware of malnutrition. Making people aware of this issue was the biggest obstacle. Only 50 per cent of the children could be covered in this. There were many challenges, including the lack of interest of the community towards malnutrition, severe lack of coordination among all the departments concerned, lack of capacity among the personnel engaged in this work, and lack of attention to prevention.

Malnutrition is an invisible social problem. The intensity of its damage is very slow. That is why people do not see it nor does it suddenly create trouble. It is a curse. If the child remains malnourished right from the mother's womb till 5 years of age, then after 5 years the deficiency in the body resulting from malnutrition cannot be overcome. Therefore, this period has its own importance in life.

The following are the damages done by malnutrition:

1. Malnutrition accounts for 53 per cent of deaths in children up to 5 years of age.
2. The physical and intellectual capacity of the child decreases.
3. This hinders the development of the country.

डी.एम. ने आकर ऐसा चमत्कार कर दिया।
सब बेखबर थे, सबको खबरदार कर दिया।
बाँदा जिले से उसने कुपोषण घटा दिया।
सेहत के साथ जीने का रास्ता दिखा दिया॥

—नज़रे आलम 'नज़र बाँदवी'

Banda nutrition campaign: objectives

1. To make nutrition a public health issue and to make it a priority to eliminate malnutrition.
2. Strengthening the district health and ICDS system for detection, prevention and management of undernutrition among children.
3. To create awareness and create an enhanced caregiving capacity among all concerned to improve the process of child feeding and care.
4. In order to accelerate the efforts to eradicate malnutrition across the country, the central government also launched a nutrition program in 2018.

Integrated Management of Severe Acute Malnutrition (IMSAM)

Based on a UNICEF report

Malnutrition in children is a very serious problem. According to the World Health Organization, medical management of SAM children is essential and about 10 per cent of SAM children have a medical complication and hospitalization of such SAM children is mandatory. The remaining 90 per cent of SAM children can be managed through community-level energy and nutrient-rich diets by providing necessary medical tests and antibiotics and micronutrients.

Current Status of SAM management in India: The policy and program related to the management of SAM children in India currently only provides in-patient care, which covers only 1–2 per cent of SAM children through nutritional rehabilitation centres (NRCs) annually.

Pilot Project in Uttar Pradesh: In collaboration with UNICEF, a pilot project was implemented in Banda district's Naraini block in the year 2018 for the identification and management of SAM children. The main objective of this project was to showcase the model of the system of identification, referral, and management of SAM children. Out of 270 Anganwadi centers in the Naraini block, 50 Anganwadi centers were selected as model sites. SAM children were weighed at the beginning and end of each phase by the Anganwadi worker through the project team, and their condition was recorded and additional information related to their diet and medical condition was also collected.

During these sessions, nutritional methods using appropriate nutrition and local nutritious food items like peanuts, sesame, jaggery, oil/ghee, vegetables, etc., were explained. The children were given tasty food made of nutritious ingredients at the centres, once. Apart from this, during these sessions, parents were also given counselling related to nutrition, health and hygiene of the child.

Pilot project results: Complete improvement (SAM to normal) was observed in about 38 per cent of SAM children and partial improvement in 24 per cent of children. The monitoring data of the pilot shows that the SAM children who had taken the antibiotics and micronutrients received from the medical center, and their parents had given the children the food made from the nutritious and other food items displayed during the child nutrition session, as per the advice of the Anganwadi worker showed more improvement. Similarly, in an another community-based SAM children management pilot project conducted in India (Bhandari, 2018), children from one of the 3 groups of SAM children were given nutritious home-cooked food. About 42 per cent of the SAM children in that group showed an improvement, which was comparable to Naraini Pilot Project.

The scale of the Banda Pilot Project: The program was launched under the Nutrition Program, on 26th January 2019, in the entire district under the name of 'Banda Nutrition Program'.

Main stages

- Formation of task force under the chairmanship of DM in Banda nutrition program.
- Coordination of departments—Mining Department, Health Department, Women and Child Development, Panchayati Raj, SRLM, etc.
- A nodal officer for the program was appointed to increase coordination and run the activities without any interruption.
- Financial support for the program—Mining Department, Beti Bachao Beti Padhao, Health Department and ICDS.
- Non-governmental organizations like UNICEF were associated with the program.

- Seven hundred weighing machines, inch tapes, scales, reporting formats, community weight growth charts, counselling tools (for all anganwadis) medicines and micronutrients (for all health centres)—funding support by VHNSC funds and funds of non-governmental institutions.
- Capacity-building of officers, employees (ASHA/ANM/ Anganwadi workers) of health, ICDS departments, 1,500 Anganwadi workers, 236 ANMs, financial support by Beti Bachao Beti Padhao funds and funds of non-government organizations.
- Standard operating procedures and roles and responsibilities were set for each department.
- Weekly review of the progress of the programme by the DM and monthly review of all the related departments.

Implementation

- From February to May 2019, the first phase of the programme was implemented in all the Anganwadi centres of the district.

  Under this, in the month of February, a two-day campaign was conducted in all Anganwadi centres to measure the weight and height of children below five years of age.
- All the malnourished and SAM/MAM children identified in the campaign were enrolled for the first phase of three months. The first phase was implemented from March to May, in which child nutrition sessions were organised at Anganwadi centres during 1–7 March 1–7 April, and 13–19 May. These child nutrition sessions were financed by the District Mining fund. Apart from this, necessary medical treatment was provided free of cost to the SAM children at the health centre or nutritional rehabilitation centre.

The results of the first stage

1. **Screening and enrolment**
   - A total of 1,27,903 children were weighed (49 per cent of the total population of children under the age of 5)
   - A total of 1,16,176 children's height was measured (45 per cent of the total population of children under the age of five)
   - Number and percentage of total SAM/MAM children—6,649 (5.7 per cent)
   - Number and percentage of total SAM children—2,840 (2.4 per cent)
   - Total number and percentage of MAM children—3,809 (3.3 per cent)
2. **Result of the programme**
   - SAM and MAM children who were in the normal category in the category of weight relative to height—1,659 (25 per cent)
   - SAM children who were in the normal range in the height relative to weight category—484 (17 per cent)

Improvements in the next phase after the challenges of the first phase

- In the first phase, only 49 per cent of children were screened.
- There was less cooperation in the first phase, mainly because the families did not give importance to the problem of malnutrition. The program's lack of IEC and community mobilization activities and strategy emerged.
- In the first phase, higher priority was given to the management-related activities in malnourished children than the activities related to the prevention of malnutrition.

जन–जन की भागीदारी, सुपोषण के लिए है जरूरी : हीरा लाल

पोषण माह में हर स्तर पर हो सुपोषित समाज के निर्माण की तैयारी

सरिता प्रवाह ब्यूरो

लखनऊ। देश के सम्पूर्ण विकास में एक स्वस्थ समाज की अहम भूमिका होती है। इसके लिए जरूरी है कि सबसे पहले हम अपने गाँव को ही कुपोषण मुक्त बनाने की शुरुआत करें। इसके लिए यह एक सुनहरा मौका भी है क्योंकि सितम्बर माह को राष्ट्रीय पोषण माह के रूप में पूरे देश में मनाया जा रहा है।

यह पोषण अभियान एक कार्यक्रम न होकर एक जन आन्दोलन और समग्र भागीदारी के रूप में है। इस कार्यक्रम को सही मायने में धरातल पर उतारने के लिए जरूरी है कि स्थानीय पंचायत प्रतिनिधि, स्कूल प्रबन्धन समितियां, सरकारी विभाग, सामाजिक संगठन आगे आएं और सामूहिक प्रयास से देश को कुपोषण मुक्त बनाएं। यह बातें राष्ट्रीय स्वास्थ्य मिशन-उत्तर प्रदेश के अपर मिशन निदेशक डॉ. हीरा लाल ने राष्ट्रीय पोषण माह की शुरुआत पर कहीं।

डॉ. हीरा लाल ने कहा कि इस अभियान की सफलता इसी में निहित है कि घर-घर पोषण का त्योहार मनाया जाए। पंचायत प्रतिनिधि हर बच्चे, किशोर-किशोरी, गर्भवती व धात्री महिला को निर्धारित पोषण सेवा का लाभ प्रदान करने के साथ उस बारे में जागरूक बनाएं। यह सुनिश्चित करें कि गाँव की किसी भी लड़की की शादी 18 साल की उम्र से पहले न हो, क्योंकि कम उम्र में शादी से जहाँ एक ओर उस लड़की का स्वास्थ्य प्रभावित होता है वहीं जल्दी माँ बनने से कुपोषित बच्चे को जन्म देने की पूरी गुंजाइश भी रहती है। यह भी सुनिश्चित करें कि हर गर्भवती का संस्थागत प्रसव हो क्योंकि इसी में जच्चा-बच्चा की सुरक्षा निहित है।

खुले में शौच पर पूरी तरह रोक लगाएं और लोगों को बीमारियों से बचाएं। इसके अलावा गाँव के लोगों को साग-सब्जी व पौधों को लगाने के लिए प्रेरित करें ताकि परिवार को हरी साग-सब्जियां आसानी से मिल सकें। सुरक्षित पेयजल और स्वच्छ वातावरण का भी ख्याल रखें। ग्राम स्वास्थ्य स्वच्छता व पोषण दिवस (वीएचएसएनडी) की नियमित बैठक से इन कामों को आसान बनाया जा सकता है।

आंगनबाड़ी व आशा कार्यकर्ता दिखाएं समझदारी

सुपोषण की अलख जगाने में आंगनबाड़ी और आशा कार्यकर्ता महत्वपूर्ण जिम्मेदारी निभा सकती हैं। इसके लिए जरूरी है कि आंगनबाड़ी कार्यकर्ता केंद्र के साथ ही गृह भ्रमण के दौरान समुचित पोषण सम्बन्धी परामर्श नियमित रूप से प्रदान करें। बच्चों का नियमित और पूर्ण टीकाकरण सुनिश्चित करें, बच्चों के शारीरिक और बौद्धिक विकास की निगरानी करें और गर्भवती व नवजात शिशुओं की निगरानी के लिए नियमित गृह भ्रमण पर जोर दें। बच्चों का नियमित रूप से वजन करें और एमसीपी कार्ड कार्ड में दर्ज करें और लाल घेरे में आते ही निकटतम केंद्र पर जाने के लिए प्रेरित करें। इसी तरह से आशा कार्यकर्ता हर गर्भवती की प्रसव पूर्व जाँच कराएं और संस्थागत प्रसव के लिए प्रेरित करें। नवजात शिशु की देखभाल व धात्री महिला की निगरानी के लिए निर्धारित गृह भ्रमण सुनिश्चित करें। अति कुपोषित बच्चों और कम वजन के बच्चों की निगरानी के लिए हर महीने गृह भ्रमण कर और जरूरी परामर्श दें।

स्कूल प्रबंधन समितियां व सामुदायिक रेडियो स्टेशन भी निभाएं जिम्मेदारी

स्कूल प्रबन्धन समितियां किशोर-किशोरियों को एनीमिया से बचाव के प्रति जागरूक बनाएं और बच्चों को साफ-सफाई व स्वच्छता के प्रति सजग और जवाबदेह बनाएं ताकि उनका समग्र विकास सुनिश्चित हो सके। इसी तरह सामुदायिक रेडियो स्टेशन भी पोषण के विभिन्न पहलुओं से सम्बन्धित कार्यक्रम तैयार कर उसे प्रसारित कर एक बड़ा बदलाव ला सकते हैं। कृषि से उपलब्ध स्थानीय पोषक आहारों के बारे में जागरूकता फैलाने की उनकी मुहिम भी रंग ला सकती है। इसके अलावा खाना बनाने की स्थानीय विधि, भोजन की कैलोरी में वृद्धि तथा पौष्टिक आहार पर कार्यक्रम प्रस्तुत कर सुपोषित समाज बनाने में मददगार साबित हो सकते हैं।

Community participation was essential for the success of the program. For this, in the second phase, the strategy of '90+ per cent' was worked out to make the program a mass movement. Under this, the target of coverage of six indicators of activities in the program was fixed at 90+ per cent. Apart from this, several activities like media plan, IEC plan, and sensitization of various stakeholders were proposed under this comprehensive strategy.

❑

3.5

Prison Reforms

There is a general belief that prison is meant for punishment, whereas, in reality, a prison is a correctional home. Here, every attempt is made to reform the criminal and help him lead a good life.

As a District Magistrate, Banda, it was my responsibility to inspect the jail every month along with the superintendent of police and the District Judge. All three people check whether all the arrangements in the jail are according to the rules or not and that there is nothing amiss. I had heard a lot about Mrs Kiran Bedi,

India's first woman IPS, who did good work for prison reforms. Because of this, there was a curiosity in my mind. If Bediji could carry out good reforms in prison, why couldn't a District Magistrate do so?

The main problems of the prisoner:

1. Guilt
2. Not able to use the time as per interest
3. Lack of anyone to listen to their problems and give solutions
4. Frustrated and desperate life and routine.

In a way, a jail is like a village and the barracks are like its mohallas.

When I went for inspection for the first time, I found 18 barracks in the jail with prisoner capacity of 567 whereas the number of prisoners were 900. Female prisoners' capacity was 30 whereas the number of women prisoners was 33.

Smile was noticeably absent from the faces of the prisoners. Everyone seemed desperate and disappointed. All the faces looked dark because of the pain, the agony and the trouble. I didn't like all that. I was upset. There was an atmosphere of despair in the entire jail.

I decided to change it. I thought that 'we would adopt innovative activities and make Banda jail, the best.' I spoke to Mr R. K. Singh, the jail superintendent. It was decided that first of all, efforts should be made for improving the health of the people. Mr Ramesh Singh Rajput, a yoga teacher, was sent to the prison. He was to select four prisoners from each barrack and teach yoga to them for a week. After learning yoga, these people would practice yoga every morning in their respective barracks. This idea was very effective. All the prisoners started getting up in the morning and started doing yoga in their respective barracks. The mornings thus turned out to be pleasant and productive. Everyone's health improved. People did not fall sick so often. Prevention is better than cure. Yoga is the best and simplest means of prevention.

I went for inspection again the next month and started two new activities. First—everyday sports and second— cultural activities.

We asked all the prisoners about their interest in sports. Various groups were formed according to the games. Everyone started playing the games of their choice in their respective groups during the day. They started to play sports like football, kabaddi, volleyball, tug of war, etc., every day. Due to this, people used their time in a positive way. This brought happiness to the prisoners and their health also improved.

In Banda, there was good knowledge and attachment to cultural activities among the public. There was a stage in the jail and all the prisoners used to sit in front of it and perform a program. It was decided that a cultural program would be held once in a week, for two to three hours. Some of the prisoners would perform and the rest would watch. That would give every prisoner a chance to show their skills. There would be two to three hours of entertainment per week. That would gradually eliminate the negative energy and increase the positive energy in people, and frustration and despair would decrease.

Yoga, sports, cultural programs, and cleanliness drives created a good atmosphere. Prisoners who were interested in cleanliness and valued cleanliness were engaged in this work. Regular cleaning was started every day. The cleanliness drive was undertaken every week. The clean environment made the prison premises energetic and delightful.

When I again went for the inspection in the next month, I started art and handicrafts activities. Necessary materials were made available to the prisoners. They painted on the walls of the jail. They made good works of art. The prison environment became better and colourful. The prison complex looked beautiful and charming.

Inside the prison, various types of nests were built on the trees for birds, which attracted them. The prisoners were given the responsibility of feeding the birds with their leftover food. This increased the connection of the prison complex with nature.

Skill development programs were conducted for around 30 women prisoners, due to which they found work of their interest and enjoyed spending time in a positive way.

Proper arrangements were made for all the prisoners to celebrate all the festivals with full enthusiasm. I personally used to participate in Holi, Diwali and Eid celebrations. Every festival was a day of celebration.

Till now, there was no dairy in any of the 72 prisons of the state. I started a dairy for the first time in Banda. District Judge Shri Radheshyam Yadav inaugurated it. Vermi compost was made from cow dung and used in the prison farm. The milk was used for the prisoners. Those prisoners who were interested in dairy used to operate it.

जेल में हुनर साझा कर बंदी गढ़ रहे प्रतिभा की इबारत

लखनऊ जिला जेल में आज होगा तिनका-तिनका सम्मान समारोह

दो महिला बंदी भी आयोजन में की गई शामिल

Water conservation was also carried out throughout the jail premises. A pond was also dug. Many people voluntarily took part in water conservation.

Magazines, newspapers, books, etc., were provided to all the prisoners according to their interests so that they could utilize their time for readings.

Tulsi and neem plants were used as medicine on the campus. Prisoners interested in the agricultural activities were made in-charge of the farm on the jail premises and organic farming was undertaken. The farm was divided into four parts, each with an in-charge and a co-in-charge. All help was provided through the agriculture officer and horticulture officer.

We renovated a park in front of the jail. This was a good facility for the workers in the jail as well as the people coming to visit the prisoners. Placing an officer on duty every day, listening to the problems of each prisoner in front of his lawyer and family, and trying to give solutions was very effective. Everyone was properly represented. It helped in reducing the sentences of many prisoners and getting them bailed quickly.

Jail Administration, Uttar Pradesh formed a committee and got all the work of all the jails evaluated. For doing the best job in all the tasks, Banda was rewarded as the best prison.

Now most of the time of prisoners was spent productively according to their interests, passions and needs. All of them started living as neighbours and family in a village. They were happy. Shri U. P. Singh, secretary, Jal Shakti, Government of India visited the jail. Shri Anand Kumar, Inspector General of Jail, Government of Uttar Pradesh conducted the inspection. Prof. Nitin Singh, IIM Ranchi, also inspected the jail and wrote a research paper on reforms.

महानिरीक्षक कारागार प्रशासन एवं सुधार सेवायें, उत्तर प्रदेश

प्रशंसा-पत्र

माह जुलाई, 2017 से जून, 2019 की अवधि में कारागार की सुरक्षा व अनुशासन व्यवस्था को सुदृढ़ रखने के कारण किसी भी प्रकार की अप्रिय घटना घटित नहीं हुई। इस अवधि में विभाग में संचालित विभिन्न योजनाओं का बेहतर ढंग से संचालन किया गया, जिसके लिये ''जिला कारागार बाँदा'' को ''सर्वोत्तम कारागार'' चयनित करते हुये कारागार पर तैनात समस्त कार्मिकों की प्रशंसा की जाती है तथा अपेक्षा की जाती है कि वे भविष्य में भी इसी प्रकार पूर्ण मनोयोग, कर्त्तव्यनिष्ठा एवं परिश्रम से अपने दायित्वों का निर्वहन करेंगे।

(आनन्द कुमार)
पुलिस महानिदेशक/महानिरीक्षक
कारागार प्रशासन एवं सुधार सेवायें, उत्तर प्रदेश।

लखनऊ
दिनांक : 02 अगस्त, 2019

Ms Vartika Nanda, prison reform activist and prison reformer also visited the jail and gave suggestions. The *'Tinka-Tinka'* award was also given to Banda jail by them for prison reform.

I derived great pleasure from this work. This is a rare task. Unfortunately, the officers generally do not pay adequate attention to this aspect, but I was inspired by Mrs Bedi's work in Tihar and I was successful, too.

कुछ काम पर लगे हैं तो कुछ अपने खेल में।
जीवन सुधर रहा है अब कैदी का जेल में।
मिलती नहीं मिसाल कहीं इसके मेल की।
काया पलटकर रख दी है डी.एम. ने जेल की।

—नज़रे आलम 'नज़र बाँदवी

❑

3.6

Save Trees Campaign

Everyone is familiar with the difficulties and even loss of lives due to lack of oxygen during the Corona period.

People realized the importance of oxygen in their lives. In general, we tend to forget the value of trees, that support our lives by producing oxygen.

Since the independence of the country, the tree plantation program is run every year during the rainy season. Preparations are made for the plantation in May–June and then as soon as the rains start, the plantation is done at the beginning of the rainy season. For this work, a committee is formed in each district

जनांदोलन बनाएं पौधरोपण अभियान

डीएम ने कहा-जलवायु परिवर्तन रोकने के लिए पौधरोपण जरूरी

अमर उजाला ब्यूरो

बांदा। पौधरोपण अभियान को जनांदोलन बनाया जाए। प्रदूषण और जलवायु परिवर्तन को रोकने के लिए पौधरोपण बहुत जरूरी है। वृक्षों के बिना सृष्टि की कल्पना नहीं की जा सकती। यह उद्गार जिलाधिकारी हीरा लाल ने अपने कैंप कार्यालय में आयोजित पौधरोपण उत्सव में व्यक्त किए।

बुधवार को पौधरोपण से पूर्व डीएम ने मंत्रोच्चारण के बीच पूजा-अर्चना की। आवास में खोदे गए तालाब किनारे आंवला, नीम, सहजन आदि पौधे रोपे। उन्होंने कई विभागों के अधिकारियों और कर्मचारियों से कहा कि जिले को हरा-भरा बनाने के लिए सभी कम से कम दो पौधे लगाएं। एसपी गणेश साहा ने कहा कि भावी पीढ़ी को शुद्ध वातावरण उपलब्ध कराने के लिए पौधरोपण की जरूरत है। एडीएम संतोष बहादुर सिंह, एडीएम (न्यायिक) संजय कुमार, सिटी मजिस्ट्रेट प्रदीप कुमार, एसडीएम संदीप कुमार, [illegible] श्रीवास्तव, मंसूर अहमद, मुख्य कोषाधिकारी विनोद कुमार, उप निदेशक सूचना भूपेंद्र सिंह यादव भी शामिल रहे।

पौधरोपण से पूर्व पूजा-अर्चना करते डीएम और एसपी। अमर उजाला

under the chairmanship of the District Magistrate. The divisional forest officer is its Member Secretary. All departments are its members. Since 1995, I have also been undertaking tree plantation as a part of this system, but I have not found any success. Why did tree cover not increasing through plantation? This question haunted me constantly. When I started looking for the answer I personally felt that our plan needed a change which is not effective. Accordingly, we started thinking new name of the campaign. Its new name was *'Ped Jiao Abhiyan (Keep the Tree Alive Campaign)'*. We plant trees, but most of them do not survive and die. Plant a tree and help it live. I shifted my focus from planting the tree to 'Keep the Tree Alive'. Keeping trees alive automatically involves planting trees. Planting trees is an unfinished activity. Keeping trees alive is the whole process of tree plantation. To turn this thought into reality, I devised a concrete strategy. I started working towards creating an attachment to trees in people's minds and that they should take care of them and keep them alive.

First, we started the scheme of 'Ped Prasad'. We took the support of religious beliefs. As per our beliefs and faith, we go to places of worship like temples, mosques, gurudwaras, churches, etc. People often offer sweets, flowers, leaves, sheets (chadar), etc., as prasad. The prasad is offered to God by the priests and out of the prasad offered earlier, which is called bhog, they give us prasad. We connected the same process to the tree. A plant should also be offered along with sweets, cloth, fruits, flowers and leaves as prasad. People will get the plants offered in the past in the form of prasad. If people plant it, they will take care because now the faith of the temple has been attached to this plant, and now there is the power of religious faith attached to this plant. That is why people have an unbreakable attachment to the plant received from the place of worship and they would try their best to keep it alive.

डीएम शुरू कर रहे नायाब अभियान, श्रद्धालुओं को बांटे जाएंगे पौधे, सीडीओ की अगुवाई में बनी कमेटी

हरियाली भी धर्म, सीख देंगे धार्मिक स्थल

बहुत जल्द मंदिर, मस्जिद-मजार और गुरुद्वारे आदि धार्मिक स्थलों पर एक पहल दिखाई देगी। यहां आने वालों को पौधा दिया जाएगा। संदेश दिया जाएगा कि हरियाली बढ़ाना भी एक धर्म है। श्रद्धालु इन पौधों को रोपेंगे।

जिले में हरियाली बढ़ाने के लिए जिलाधिकारी हीरा लाल यह नायाब अभियान शुरू कर रहे हैं। सीडीओ की अगुवाई में तैयार की गई यह टीम सभी पुजारियों-मुतवल्लियों या अन्य धार्मिक गुरुओं से सीधे संपर्क कर पौधा वितरण का दायित्व सौंपेगी।

जिले में वन क्षेत्र महज 2.50 फीसद है जबकि मानक के अनुसार इसे 33 फीसद होना चाहिए। हर वर्ष लाखों पौधे रोपित होते हैं, लेकिन देखरेख न होने से सूख जाते हैं या फिर जानवरों का निवाला बन जाते हैं। ऐसे में हरियाली बढ़ाने के लिए जिलेवासियों को धार्मिक भावना से जोड़ने का निर्णय लिया गया है। जिलाधिकारी ने इस अभियान की रूपरेखा तैयार कर ली है। धार्मिक स्थल अभियान का मुख्य केंद्र होंगे। जिलाधिकारी ने जिला स्तरीय अधिकारियों को इसका दायित्व सौंपा है। डीएम के साथ ही मुख्य विकास अधिकारी इसके नोडल होंगे। क्षेत्रीय वनाधिकारी जुनैद अहमद पौधे उपलब्ध कराएंगे। पौधे वन विभाग की नर्सरी में तैयार हो रहे हैं।

तीन दिन में तैयार होगा प्रस्ताव : जिलाधिकारी ने बताया कि धार्मिक स्थलों से पौधों का वितरण करने के लिए कमेटी प्रस्ताव तैयार करेगी। इसके लिए तीन दिन का निर्धारित किया है। कमेटी धर्मगुरुओं, धर्मस्थल प्रबंधकों, स्थानीय दुकानदारों के साथ [illegible] करेगी। इस दौरान प्रस्ताव प्रस्तु[illegible] सहमति पत्र प्रस्तुत किया [illegible] अभियान अनवरत चलेगा।

इन पौधों को प्रमुखता
अभी इस समय फूलों का मौसम चल रहा है, इसलिए गेंदा, गुलाब, तुलसी सहित कई शोभाकार पौधों अभियान में शामिल किया जाएगा। इसके बाद अभियान में नीम, पीपल और बरगद के पौधों को प्राथमिकता दी जाएगी।

For this new innovative approach and step, we first had a meeting with the main priests of temple, mosque, gurudwara and convinced them about our new innovative approach. They liked our idea and agreed to cooperate. After that, we held a meeting with the management committees of the places of worship so that we could get everyone's support. Arrangements were made for the donation of five hundred plants from the Forest Department for each place of worship. We informed them that we should start by offering *'Ped Prasad'* so that a new environment is created. I personally went to the places of worship and distributed saplings. The officers and members were appointed for the review of the plantation drive in places of worship in the entire district. It was widely publicized. The starting was good and gradually showing results. The new idea of *'Ped Prasad'* began to flourish.

श्रद्धालुओं को प्रसाद में दिए पौधे

गुरु गोबिंद सिंह जयंती पर अफसरों ने बांटे लोगों को पौधे, पर्यावरण की दिलाई शपथ

श्रद्धालुओं को पेड़ प्रसाद बांटते वन समेत कई विभागों के अधिकारी और गुरुद्वारा में रुमाला चढ़ाती सिख महिलाएं और ग्रंथी अमरलाल। अमर उजाला

अमर उजाला ब्यूरो

बांदा। गुरु गोबिंद सिंह की जयंती पर गुरुद्वारा आए श्रद्धालुओं को अबकी पूड़ी-मिठाई के साथ एक नया प्रसाद मिला। यह प्रसाद पौधे थे। डीएम हीरालाल ने अपने हाथों से श्रद्धालुओं को तकरीबन सौ फुलवारी (गेंदा और गुलाब) के पौधे सौंपे और श्रद्धालुओं से इन्हें अपने घरों में लगाने का वादा कराया। साथ ही पेड़ों का महत्व बताया। कहा कि जल और जंगल दोनों जरूरी हैं। इसीलिए धार्मिक स्थलों में श्रद्धालुओं को पेड़-प्रसाद अभियान चलाया गया है। उन्होंने श्रद्धालुओं को शपथ भी दिलाई। बताया कि 22 मंदिर, एक मस्जिद तथा गुरुद्वारा में यह अभियान शुरू हो चुका है। इस अवसर पर [illegible]

गुरु गोबिंद सिंह की जयंती मनाई

बांदा। सिखों के 10वें और अंतिम गुरु गोबिंद सिंह की 354वीं जयंती गुरुद्वारे में धूमधाम से मनाई गई। [illegible]

After this, the children from classes 9 to 12 were prepared for tree plantation. Through the principal of the school, the class teacher got the children to dig pits in the space available to them. The pots were arranged. When the children were ready to plant saplings and keep them alive, about 50,000 saplings were distributed to them as per their demand by 8 urban bodies. This inculcated the love for plants in the minds of students. For about 2 months, students were given all the information about the plantation through various activities. We created a passion among in them and gave them saplings so that they could plant them and keep them alive.

प्रसाद निषाद ने ध्वजा रोहण किया।

डीएम ने छात्र-छात्राओं को पौधरोपण के लिए किया प्रेरित।

Many people would invite me on their birthday. One Mr Rahul Jain met me and said that every year, he used to plant hundred saplings on his birthday. I took up his idea. I informed all that I would visit their place who planted at least hundred saplings on his birthday. This idea clicked and people slowly started doing it to invite me on their birthday and create an atmosphere for tree plantation. If the District Magistrate had to attend anyone's birthday, then a hundred saplings had to be planted. The message began to spread.

Often people used to invite me to weddings. If the District Magistrate attends someone's marriage, then their status and social prestige rise. I said that if anyone gifted at least a hundred saplings to the guests, I would attend their wedding. This idea also worked. I attended many weddings.

Many people love to decorate their houses with trees and plants. I found such houses and visited their homes. They were given a letter of appreciation for this good work. This created a feeling among the people that they should decorate their houses with plants and invite the district magistrate home. Good work was recognised.

मंदिर, मसजिद, गुरुद्वारे को, होली को, दीवाली को।
धर्म, कर्म से जोड़ दिया है डी.एम. ने हरियाली को।
दुनिया में हर काम से पहले इतना हर इनसान करे।
सबको जीवन देने वाले, पौधों का सम्मान करे।

—नज़रे आलम 'नज़र बाँदवी'

बरातियों को पौधों का तोहफा

संवाद न्यूज एजेंसी

बांदा। विभिन्न अवसरों और धार्मिक अनुष्ठानों में चल रहे पेड़ प्रसाद अभियान के तहत सोमवार को शहर के एक वैवाहिक समारोह में डीएम हीरा लाल ने वर-वधू सहित दोनों पक्षों के लोगों को पौधों का तोहफा दिया।

कहा कि इसे घर में संरक्षित करें और शुद्ध आक्सीजन हासिल करें। इंदिरा नगर में सुरेश कुमार गुप्ता की पुत्री ज्योति गुप्ता का विवाह था। कन्या पक्ष की सहमति पर डीएम हीरालाल अफसरों के साथ विवाहोत्सव में शामिल हुए। वर-वधू को बधाई के साथ पौध भेंट किए। उनके अलावा अन्य लोगों को

वर-वधू को पौध का तोहफा देते डीएम हीरालाल। संवाद

गमले सहित 151 पौध सौंपे। कहा कि जीवन का अस्तित्व पेड़-पौधों बिना संभव नहीं है। जिस आक्सीजन से हमें जीवन मिल रहा है वह इन्हीं पेड़ों से मिलती है। इस अवसर पर डीएफओ संजय अग्रवाल, सदर तहसीलदार अवधेश कुमार निगम, रिटायर्ड सीडीओ हीरालाल, प्रशंसा गुप्ता, रिटायर्ड रेंजर जुनैद अहमद और मैग्जीन एडीटर गुरुशरन धनजन आदि उपस्थित रहे।

I used to be invited as the chief guest during the annual functions in schools. I kept a condition that if any school donated at least hundred saplings to the students and parents, I would visit that school. This experiment was also successful.

The purpose was to connect people with the trees in some way or the other so that they could attach to the trees. The media liked this innovation very much. They gave a lot of publicity and took this idea to the common man.

❑

3.7

Yoga Keeps You Healthy

बाँदा में योग के अभिनव प्रयोग, गाँव-गाँव में हो रहा है अब योग।

Prevention is better than cure

Yoga is prevention. To get well by taking medicine when sick is the cure. Why should we fall sick? This is what we have to think about and take action. Daily yoga is the only way and means by which we can remain healthy. Everyone's focus should be shifted to prevention from cure. It is our goal to keep everyone healthy, energetic and efficient by instilling yoga in their body and mind.

—District Magistrate Dr Heera Lal, IAS

The word 'yoga' is derived from the Sanskrit root yuj, which means to unite. It is one of the 6 schools of thought, whose pioneer is Maharishi Patanjali. According to Maharishi Patanjali, controlling the tendencies of the mind is yoga. When the tendencies of the mind are calm, then the mind becomes calm. When the mind is calm, then the self is revealed; otherwise, this fickle mind keeps on making us wander outside. When we are focused on ourselves, we are relaxed and healthy. According to Shrimad Bhagwat Geeta, yoga is a skill of performing yoga actions. Yoga gives us the ability to stay the same in every situation. According to the Garud Puran, yoga is the ultimate medicine for a person who is affected by the threefold heat of physical, divine and material. The underlying concept behind yoga is physical, mental, spiritual and character development.

As a District Magistrate, I decided that yoga would be taken to every village. For this, I made a concrete action plan, as a part of which I wrote a letter to each department stating that it was mandatory to do yoga in every department of the district; its title was, *'DM ki chitthi aayi hai—swasthya aur khushahali ka sandesha laayi hai'*.

I want to see every person in my district healthy and happy. That's why I have decided to take yoga to the masses in a simple, easy and 'no-cost' way.

दैनिक जागरण, झाँसी, 16, नवम्बर

योगा को जनपद का बनाया जाये मॉडल: डीएम

डीएम ने सभी अस्पतालों व एएनएम सेंटरों में योगा कराने के दिये निर्देश

बाँदा : जनपद के सभी स्वास्थ्य केन्द्रों व एएनएम सेण्टरों में योगा कराया जाये ताकि बनाये गये 75 योगा सेंटर माडल के रूप में विकसित हो सके। जिलाधिकारी हीरा लाल ने यह निर्देश अपने कैम्प कार्यालय में नेशनल मेंटल हेल्थ प्रोग्राम की समीक्षा बैठक के दौरान मुख्य चिकित्सा अधिकारी को दिये। उन्होंने कहा कि जनपद में जितने भी सीएचसी व पीएचसी के अलावा 288 एएनएम सेंटरों में योगा प्रारम्भ कराया जाये। उन्होंने मुख्य चिकित्सा अधिकारी को निर्देशित करते हुए कहा कि योगा की एक मोहर बनवायी जाये और लाल इंक से जितने भी ओपीडी में पर्चे बनाये जाये उन सभी पर्चों में यह मोहर लगायी जाये। मोहर में करो योग रहो निरोग जैसे स्लोगन का प्रयोग किया जाये। उन्होंने चिकित्सकों से यह भी कहा कि जितने भी मरीज आये उन सभी को योग के प्रति जागरूक करें और उन्हें बतायें कि योग से वह निरोगी जीवन जी सकते है। इसके साथ साथ जिलाधिकारी ने वाल राइटिंग और बैनर्स के माध्यम से भी इसका प्रचार प्रसार करने पर जोर दिया। उन्होंने सीएमओ से कहा कि वह सभी स्वास्थ्य केन्द्रों में योग से सम्बन्धित स्लोगन चिकित्सालयों में लिखवायें ताकि लोगों में जागरूकता आ सके। उन्होंने कहा कि जनपद में जो 75 योगा सेंटर चलाये जायेंगे उनमें मानसिक रोगियों को योगा कराया जायेगा और बीच-बीच में मानसिक रोग जागरूकता शिविर भी आयोजित किये जाये और लोगों को जागरूक किया जाये।

बाँदा : कैम्प कार्यालय में नेशनल मेंटल हेल्थ प्रोग्राम की समीक्षा बैठक लेते डीएम।

Campaign activities: Yoga camps were organised in every block, government office, and school from 15 to 30 June 2019 as a yoga fortnight. Fifth International Yoga Day was celebrated on 21 June 2019 with full preparations at the Government Inter College Ground, Banda, which led to a wave of enthusiasm among the people. On 1 July 2019, a meeting of yoga teachers was held at the camp office, Banda, in which the role of youth in society building and the said objective were presented. Under the yoga fortnight, 32 yoga teachers of the camps were honoured with certificates. The purpose of the meeting was to make the doctors of Allopathy, Ayurvedic, Unani, Homeopathy medicine passionate about yoga so that they could take the lead in taking yoga to the masses; to prepare yoga trainers by training 4 people each in 470 villages; to train 4 teachers each in 71 basic education schools; to train 221 physical education teachers from 170 schools of secondary education; to train 1 teacher each from 93 schools of higher education. In 121 wards of 6 Nagar Panchayats and 2 Municipalities, yoga training was imparted to 4 persons from each ward.

First, 2 development blocks were selected for a pilot project—first, Barokhar Khurd and second, Naraini. On 15 July 2019, all the trainees were addressed by the District Magistrate in the Collectorate Auditorium. He said, "It is our goal to see every person always healthy and energetic. For this, we want to see the impact of yoga on health as a pilot project in the first phase; if there is a positive impact, it will be carried forward." Vishwa Yog Seva Trust team divided 58 gram panchayats of Barokhar Khurd into 5 training centres and trained them from 16 to 19 July 2019, covering 8 clusters and 10 wards. Second block, Naraini—on 26 July 2019, the District Magistrate addressed all the trainers in the Block Auditorium, Naraini. From 30 July 2019 to 2 August 2019, 83-gram panchayats and 13 clusters, 12 wards were divided into 7 training centres. After successful and encouraging implementation of the pilot project, training was given in the remaining 6 blocks, 2 municipalities and 6 nagar panchayats. The deserving yoga instructors were encouraged by citations conferred on them by the district magistrate.

The entire training was imparted by the assistant teachers of the primary school of basic education who were awarded by the governor—Yogacharya Ramesh Singh Rajput, Ramesh Singh Patel and Md. Sharif, physiotherapist and their team. On 28 July 2019, people were made aware of yoga through the demonstration by stalls of yoga and naturopathy in Kalinjar Van Mahotsav.

Preparations were made for the Grand Yoga Conference on 12 September 2019 at the GIC grounds. Prof. Dr H. R. Nagendra, Chancellor of Swami Vivekananda Yoga Anusandhan Sansthan, Bangalore, who was present along with his disciples, addressed the conference as the chief guest. He said that yoga not only cures serious diseases but it also calms the mind when we inhale and exhale slowly. He said that yoga should be included in everyone's life. Hundred yoga teachers and more than ten thousand local citizens participated in this camp. Even when it rained, people showed their enthusiasm towards the yoga campaign by doing yoga standing in water and mud and validated the importance and growing impact of the campaign.

जिंदगी को निखार देता है।
योग जीवन सँवार देता है।
योग क्या है समझ में आया है।
हमको डी.एम. ने जब बताया है।

—नज़रे आलम 'नज़र बाँदवी'

योग के लिए देश में बनेंगे डेढ़ लाख सेंटर

प्रधानमंत्री मोदी के प्रयासों से योग को अंतर्राष्ट्रीय मान्यता : डॉ. एचआर नागेंद्र, बांदा में हजारों लोगों ने किया योग

On 14 September 2019, in the Collectorate Auditorium, the district magistrate felicitated 100 Yoga Praharis and Yoga Mitras and said, “Good results are obtained only by selfless work and good intentions. If yoga is made a habit, then we will always be healthy and will not get sick. Now all of you have to run yoga programs door-to-door in every village and work selflessly with good intentions. A register should be kept in each yoga center, which will have the signatures of the people visiting there.” I also stressed on connecting more and more women of self-help groups to yoga.

Yoga training was conducted in all the offices of Banda, which was started by the collector himself from his collectorate premises. To create enthusiasm and fervour in the training, many yoga-related slogans were created, and yoga rallies were taken out.

The achievements of this first phase of training were satisfactory and encouraging. Yoga centres started functioning in the villages. Yoga was being practiced in the municipalities, in the schools of basic education, and in the colleges. Awareness about yoga also arose among the employees of the health department and they started talking about yoga treatment along with their services. The seal with 'Do yoga, stay healthy' started being used in the government papers. In each office, all the officers and employees started practicing yoga together.

अफसरों के साथ समीक्षा में बोले कि दफ्तरों में रखें सफाई

दफ्तरों में योगा अनिवार्य बढ़ेगी कार्यक्षमता : डीएम

बांदा | कार्यालय संवाददाता

कृषि क्षेत्र से जुडे विभागों की समीक्षा में डीएम हीरालाल ने कहा कि दफ्तरों की साफ सफाई रखे और हर दफ्तर में नियमित योग कराया जाए। योगा से काम की क्षमता बढती है। यदि किसानों से किसी ने धन उगाही की तो उसके खिलाफ कार्रवाई की जाएगी। साथ ही सरकारी व प्राइवेट संस्थानों में बेहतर काम करने वालों को सूची बनाई जाए ताकि उन्हें सम्मानित किया जा सके।

डीएम ने मण्डी सचिवों को निर्देश दिए कि हर मण्डी में एक तालाब खुदवाए और इसकी कार्ययोजना बनाकर शासन को पत्र भेजे। उद्यान एवं मत्स्य अधिकारी को निर्देशित करते हुए कहा कि जो सब्जियां, मछलियां, मुर्गे, अण्डें आदि खाद्य सामग्री बाहर से न मंगाकर जिले में उत्पादन की योजना बनाए। आम जन से जुड़ाव की कोशिश लगातार हर विभाग करे ताकि लोगों का सरकारी अफसरों पर विश्वास बढे। कोई कार्य किसी विभाग में लंबित नहीं रहना चाहिए। समय पर हर फरियादी की समस्या का निस्तारण किया जाए।

अब जिला स्तरीय अधिकारी अपने-अपने घरों में मिट्टी के बर्तनों का प्रयोग खाना बनाने से लेकर खाने-पीने तक करें। दफ्तर में तो प्लास्टिक का प्रयोग पूरी तरह प्रतिबंधित है। डीएम ने कहा कि स्वदेशी अपनाकर समाज को मजबूत करें।

डीएम ने बैठक में दिए निर्देश। • हिन्दुस्तान

To start the second round of training, discussions were held in the camp office. All SHG women of NRLM were trained.

योग सेण्टर में स्वयं सहायता समूह की सखियों को जोड़ें : डीएम

कहा-जनपद के 100 योग सेण्टर माडल के रूप में चलायें

बाँदा ब्यूरो। बुधवार को योग मित्रों की समीक्षा बैठक में जिलाधिकारी ने कहा कि जनपद में जितने भी योग सेन्टर है, उनमें एनआरएलएम की स्वयं सहायता समूह की सखियों को योग सेन्टर से जोड़ने का कार्य किया जाये और द्वितीय चरण का प्रशिक्षण 15 दिन के अन्दर देना सुनिश्चित करें। सेन्टर में दरी खरीदने का कार्य लेखपाल, ग्राम प्रधान, सचिव, ग्राम्य निधि से करें और योग सेन्टर में एक हाजिरी रजिस्टर भी रखा जाये।

कलेक्टरेट सभागार योग मित्रों की समीक्षा बैठक में जिलाधिकारी श्री लाल ने कहा कि जिस सेण्टर में योग कराया जायेगा। उस क्षेत्र के सभी लोगों को योग करने के लिये कहेंगे और विशेष तौर पर बीमार लोगों को योग अवश्य कराया जाये ताकि उनका स्वास्थ्य ठीक हो सके। उन्होंने यूनानी डॉक्टर को निर्देश देते हुये कहा कि योग से होने वाले लाभ से सम्बन्धित हैण्डबिल एवं बैनर बनवाकर जिलाधिकारी की तरफ से अपील छपवाई जाये। योग सेण्टर क्षेत्र के जितने भी आसपास सरकारी अधिकारी व कर्मचारी एवं रिटायर्ड कर्मी है, उन सभी की सूची तैयार कर सेण्टर से जोड़ने का कार्य करें और योग करने के प्रति प्रेरित करें। योग मित्रों से कहा कि आप सभी लोगों को एक अवसर दिया गया है। इस अवसर का सही लाभ प्राप्त करें क्योंकि यह बहुत की पुनीत कार्य है। आप उस गाँव के आदर्श पुरुष एवं आदर्श महिला के रूप में जाने जायेंगे। बस मन में एक अच्छा कार्य करने की इच्छा शक्ति होनी चाहिये। आने वाले समय में सरकार योग में बहुत लोगों को रोजगार देगी। लेकिन इसके लिये आप सभी लोगों को कठिन मेहनत के साथ-साथ डिग्री भी हासिल करनी होगी। क्योंकि इसके बिना कुछ सम्भव नहीं है। सभी लोग योग के माध्यम से ज्यादा से ज्यादा पब्लिक कनेक्टिविटि बढ़ाने का कार्य करें। जनपद में सौ योग सेण्टर है उनको माडल के रूप में चलाने का कार्य करें। जिलाधिकारी श्री लाल ने आयुर्वेद यूनानी डाक्टर पी आर वर्मा को निर्देश देते हुये कहा कि योग सम्बन्धित विलप को व्हॉट्सऐप ग्रुप के माध्यम से प्रचार-प्रसार करवायें। जिससे ज्यादा से ज्यादा लोगों को जानकारी हो सके। स्थानीय स्तर पर योग को बिना किसी अतिरिक्त संसाधन के लोकप्रिय बनाने में अपना नवाचारित सुझाव दें। उन्होंने समस्त नगर पालिका अधिशासी अधिकारियों को निर्देश दिये कि अपने-अपने नगर निकायों में योग सेण्टर प्रारम्भ कराकर योग करायें। बैठक में जिला बेसिक शिक्षाधिकारी हरिश्चन्द्रनाथ, आयुर्वेद यूनानी अधिकारी पी आर वर्मा, योग प्रशिक्षक रमेश राजपूत सहित लगभग [illegible] योग मित्र के अलावा सम्बन्धित विभाग के अधिकारी व कर्मचारी मौजूद रहे।

A meeting was organized for four yoga teachers running each yoga center with the preparation of five points, in which the District Magistrate said that:

1. It is necessary to run the yoga center automatically with public participation and increase the number of yoga centres.

2. Promotion of yoga clip, which is a short film made to promote yoga, by sending it daily to all the groups and writing a new sentence every day in the context of yoga.
3. Give your one innovative suggestion to popularize yoga at the local level without any additional resources.
4. Adding 10 other people like you and working in a team of 11 people.
5. Connect the self-help groups of women, which have been formed in each village, with the yoga center.

Yoga training was given to all the prisoners of Mandal jail, Banda, in which four prisoners from each barrack were trained as yoga trainers. Yoga is still being practiced there today.

Prevention is better than cure. We are fond of treatment. Prevention is difficult and takes a long time. So, gradually, as an easy way out, people turned away from prevention and turned to treatment, but the truth is that no one wants to get sick. The joy of being cured after getting sick, getting treatment, spending money, by suffering pain is also painful.

I realized the importance of prevention in 2014. I was then the chief development officer of Firozabad. I was suffering from back pain. I went to Sahara Hospital, Lucknow. The doctor told me that I was overweight by 10 kgs. That was the reason for my back pain. Luckily, it was not due to any disease. Mr Sarvesh Kumar Yadav, PD, told me that I should accompany him to the physiotherapist Dr Ashutosh Sharma at the Body Tuning Centre in Firozabad. Mr Yadav was also receiving treatment from Dr Sharma.

I saw that the physiotherapist Dr Sharma had good knowledge. Earlier, he practiced in Gurugram. Due to domestic issues, he came back to his home to Firozabad. I started going at six o'clock in the morning. I lost almost five kgs in two months with only preventive measures. At that time, I realised that prevention is more powerful than cure. I decided that I would keep disease away with prevention and never take medicines. I also changed my habits by taking an expert opinion on lifestyle and food habits. As a result, I did not develop any lifestyle disorders and did not have to take medicine. Now getting up at five o'clock in the morning, walking, doing yoga and exercising has become a habit.

World Yoga Day is celebrated on 21 June at the initiative of India. On this day, I like to awaken people and enlighten them about prevention. A question arose in my mind as to whether Yoga Day should be celebrated every day because yoga is a daily necessity. To make this concept a reality, I started the campaign of Yogamai Banda. This was implemented under the leadership of Mr Ramesh Singh Rajput, and his team. The teacher who was awarded the State Teacher's Award for primary.

❑

3.8

Student Development Program

All-round development of students is our need and it is also necessary. In our government schools, the focus is only on studies. Most capable people want to send their children to private schools and not government schools. Why? I found the answer. Which are the activities that take place in private schools but not in government schools? Efforts were started to implement all the activities taking place in private schools to all government schools so that the activities of government schools would be at par with those of private schools.

For that, the following steps were taken:

1. Old student association
2. Educational tour
3. NGO partnership
4. Education calendar
5. PTM
6. Mapping student interests and its development
7. Mid-day meal
8. Yoga
9. Magazine publication at development block level
10. Annual gatherings

This gave an opportunity to all the children and teachers to do new things and innovate. Progress was assessed and hurdles were removed during monthly review meetings. Special attention was paid to the working style of the block education officer. It is the most important link between making and breaking the whole system. It had such a good effect that everyone started praising the effort. A good message was sent to the general public. A letter was written to the government to implement all the successful experiments throughout Uttar Pradesh. All the programs were implemented one after the other in the entire state.

The second experiment was to give guidance to the children according to their interests and needs. A list of the fields for which the school children wanted to make preparations was made. The maximum number of students wanted to opt for engineering, medical, teaching, lawyer, acting, etc. Subject expert Mr Anmol, Prayatna Coaching, Lucknow, who runs coaching classes in Lucknow, was invited. He gave them information about how to study and what to do. This information showed the children a way forward.

आईआईटी इंजीनियर ने छात्रों को टिप्स दिए

Major Mithilesh Kumar Pandey, Principal, Adarsh Bajrang Inter College, Banda coordinated the entire program. This experiment was very fruitful. It proved to be very useful for the students who were in classes 11 and 12.

Third Innovation: Dialogue for student development

Addressing the secondary level students on the occasion of Pratibha Samman Samaroh 2019 at Adarsh Bajrang Inter College, Banda, he advised students to choose their future careers.

Earlier, information about the areas of services was not easily available. At present, setting a goal for entering any field can be done systematically.

He asked the students to set their targets with the consent of their parents and submit it in writing to their school.

कैसे भविष्य अच्छा बनेगा बता दिया।
जीवन सफल बनाने का रास्ता दिखा दिया।
डी.एम. मिले हैं जिनको भी शिक्षक के रूप में।
ठंडी सी छाँव मिल गई है उनको धूप में॥

—नज़रे आलम 'नज़र बाँदवी'

Objectives

- To motivate students to set goals.
- To make students aware of various employment opportunities.
- To motivate the students to take the right direction and make the right strategy to achieve the goal.
- To prepare students to write down the goals and communicate them to their teachers and parents.
- To make teachers, parents, and the school aware of their role in achieving these goals of the students.

जिले के युवा लिखेंगे सफलता की नई इबारत

छात्र निर्माण संवाद कार्यक्रम से करियर पर होगी निगाह

रविवार विशेष

बालिकाओं से सीधा संवाद

स्कूल-कालेजों में चल रहे छात्र-छात्रा निर्माण संवाद आयोजनों की श्रृंखला में सोमवार को सुबह डीएम हीरा लाल ने यहां राजकीय बालिका इंटर कालेज में छात्राओं से सीधे संवाद किया। उन्हें अपने जीवन का लक्ष्य निर्धारित कर उसे लिखित रूप में और माता-पिता के हस्ताक्षरों के साथ कालेज में सौंपने को कहा। छात्राओं ने डीएम से कई सवाल किए और अपनी जिज्ञासाएं पूछीं। डीएम ने उन्हें विस्तार से जवाब देकर संतुष्ट किया। प्रधानाचार्य बीना गुप्ता ने डीएम का आभार जताया। कालेज की टीचर्स उपस्थित रहीं।

Process

Under the dialogue for Student Development Program, the District Magistrate interacted directly with the students of the colleges on seven points:

1. Decide the goal of your life.
2. How high (goal) do you want to go? Have you set your target?
3. Children of today consider themselves to be smarter than parents—breaking this notion.
4. Children to take advice from their parents and set their own goals.
5. Students should give the certificate of their goal to their class teacher with the joint signatures of their mother and father.
6. Stay away from fashion and adopt simple living, high thinking.
7. Stay away from mobile and social media. Use mobile only for the purpose of studying with the help of the Google search engine.

- **Time Management:** Create a daily timetable from morning to evening and evening till night.
- During this interaction, the students were asked to set their goals, get parents' consent, and submit their goals in writing to their school.
- Based on the form of goals submitted, it was observed that four major areas were selected by most of the students:
  - (i) Engineering service
  - (ii) Medical service
  - (iii) Administrative service
  - (iv) Academic service
- A group workshop of students for each selected area was organized under the direction of the district magistrate.
- During this workshop, experts were invited and students got the opportunity to interact with them for educational guidance and communication.

Result

The students became aware of their goals. Parents and teachers became familiar with the goals of the students. Based on the goals of the students, the school took the desired action for its teaching process.

Fourth experiment: Officer for a day

While getting an education, students do a lot of theoretical studies, but they do not have practical knowledge. Therefore, in order to give them practical knowledge—e.g., how the offices are run, what work is done and how the officers work, how they will have to work when they themselves will become officers, what would be the expectations of their department and the general public from them when they are holding that post. In order to motivate them to become skilled officers, *'Ek Din ka Adhikari'* program was designed on the lines of *'Ek Din ka Mukhyamantri'*.

Objective

- Personality development.
- Enhancement in the service plan.
- Office management training.
- Observing the qualities of an officer and learning from them.
- To reduce the gap between the government and the public.
- To acquaint the students with good governance.
- Motivating and encouraging students to become officers.

Process

- In colleges, professors and students were informed about the program through letters.
- Students were asked to fill application for registration.
- To submit a two-page article on any one of the district level higher officials with whom the student wants to learn.
- Spending one day in the selected office and studying there and writing a two-page article about the study of the office.
- Staying with the desired officer for a day and learning and seeing themselves as an officer for one day after staying with the officer.
- To write an article on all the lessons learnt, in which there will be a brief description of five points:
    1. What are the departmental functions of the concerned officer?

2. How do they conduct departmental work?
3. Good things that were learnt from that officer.
4. Good things that you will apply in your life.
5. Five benefits of the program.

All the above points were compiled to make slides. A total of five slides were presented for five minutes on the specified time and date. Certificates were given to those students by the District Magistrate.

Result

- The desire to become an officer increased among the students.
- An understanding of the importance of administrative systems and posts developed in the students.
- The gap between the government and the common man decreased and the good governance system improved.
- The practical knowledge of the students increased.
- Students were inspired and motivated to become officers.

दैनिक जागरण,झाँसी,30,जनवरी

1 दिन का अधिकारी बनने वाले बच्चों को डीएम ने किया सम्मानित

बाँदा : छात्र-छात्राओं को प्रशस्ति पत्र देकर सम्मानित करते जिलाधिकारी हीरा लाल।

प्रशस्ति-पत्र पाकर खुश हुये छात्र-छात्रायें

बाँदा ब्यूरो : छात्र-छात्राओं को प्रोत्साहित करने के लिये जनपद मे चलाये जा रहे एक दिन का अधिकारी कार्यक्रम मे जिलाधिकारी ने आधा दर्जन छात्र-छात्राओं को प्रशस्ति पत्र देकर सम्मानित किया। सम्मान मिलने पर छात्र-छात्राओं के चेहरे खुशी से खिल उठे। जिलाधिकारी की पहल पर जनपद में एक दिन का अधिकारी कार्यक्रम चलाया जा रहा है। जिसमे अब तक लगभग 50 छात्र-छात्राओं द्वारा प्रमुख प्रशासनिक पदों पर एक दिन का अधिकारी बनकर अपने व्यक्तित्व का विकास करने तथा अधिकारी के कार्य एवं कर्तव्यों का अनुभव प्राप्त किया। ऐसे ही एक दिन का अधिकारी बन चुके राजकीय महिला महाविद्यालय की छात्रा वैशाली गुप्ता, पं० जवाहर लाल नेहरू महाविद्यालय के रोहित ने जिलाधिकारी के पद पर अनुभव प्राप्त किया। पं० जेएन कालेज की सौम्या ने एक दिन के लिये मुख्य विकास अधिकारी के पद का कार्यभार का अनुभव सीखा। राजकीय इंटर कालेज के हिमांशु पं० जवाहर लाल नेहरू महाविद्यालय की प्रज्ञा त्रिपाठी ने उपजिलाधिकारी, पं० जवाहर लाल नेहरू महाविद्यालय की गीता ने जिला विकास अधिकारी के कार्यों को सीखा। बुधवार को जिलाधिकारी ने कैम्प कार्यालय में एक दिन का अधिकारी समिति के सदस्यों के समक्ष पीपीटी के माध्यम से अपने अनुभव प्रस्तुत किये। इसके बाद डीएम ने इन छात्र-छात्राओं को प्रशस्ति पत्र देकर सम्मानित किया। साथ ही भविष्य में प्रशासनिक शासकीय सेवाओं से जुड़कर जनहित में कार्य करने की शुभकामनायें दी। छात्र-छात्राओं ने जिलाधिकारी आवास कैम्पस मे जल संरक्षण के लिये बनाये गये तालाब, कुओं तथा पौधरोपण के कार्यों को देखा। छात्र-छात्राओं को आवास का भ्रमण कराया गया। कार्यक्रम का संचालन सहायक निदेशक बचत आर के जैन, सहायक निदेशक सेवायोजन कौशलेन्द्र सिंह, आनन्द शुक्ला, योगेश्वर सिंह आदि मौजूद रहे।

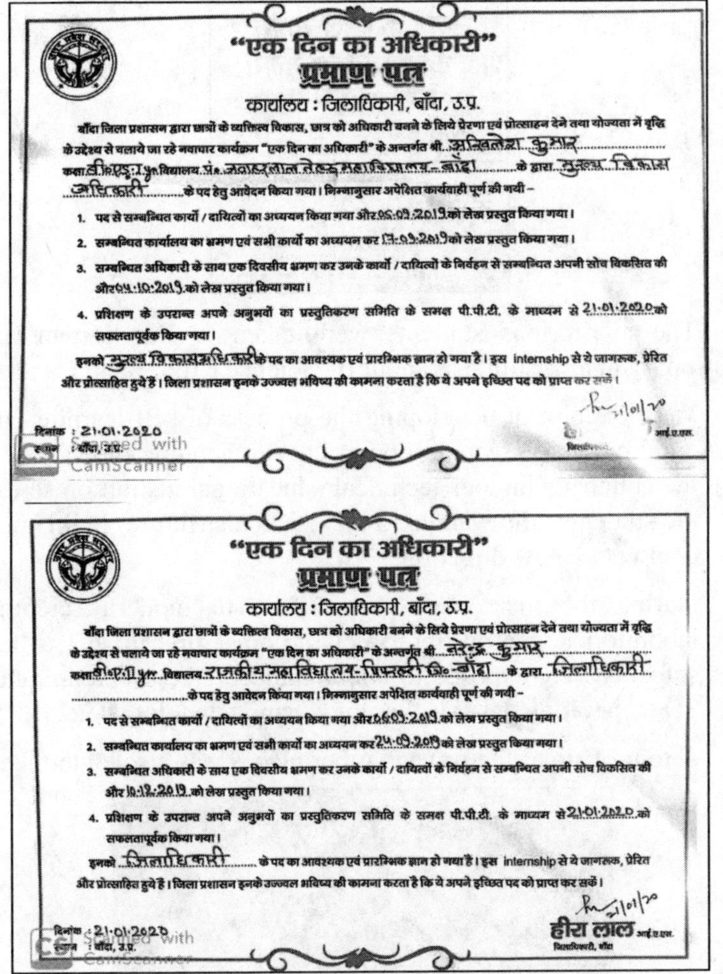

"एक दिन का अधिकारी"

प्रमाण पत्र

कार्यालय : जिलाधिकारी, बाँदा, उ.प्र.

बाँदा जिला प्रशासन द्वारा छात्रों के व्यक्तित्व विकास, छात्र को अधिकारी बनने के लिये प्रेरणा एवं प्रोत्साहन देने तथा योज्यता में वृद्धि के उद्देश्य से चलाये जा रहे नवाचार कार्यक्रम "एक दिन का अधिकारी" के अन्तर्गत श्री अखिलेश कुमार कक्षा बी.एड. I yr विद्यालय पं. जवाहरलाल नेहरू महाविद्यालय-बाँदा के द्वारा मुख्य विकास अधिकारी के पद हेतु आवेदन किया गया। निम्नानुसार अपेक्षित कार्यवाही पूर्ण की गयी -

1. पद से सम्बन्धित कार्यों / दायित्वों का अध्ययन किया गया और 06.09.2019 को लेख प्रस्तुत किया गया।
2. सम्बन्धित कार्यालय का भ्रमण एवं सभी कार्यों का अध्ययन कर 13.09.2019 को लेख प्रस्तुत किया गया।
3. सम्बन्धित अधिकारी के साथ एक दिवसीय भ्रमण कर उनके कार्यों / दायित्वों के निर्वहन से सम्बन्धित अपनी सोच विकसित की और 05.10.2019 को लेख प्रस्तुत किया गया।
4. प्रशिक्षण के उपरान्त अपने अनुभवों का प्रस्तुतिकरण समिति के समक्ष पी.पी.टी. के माध्यम से 21.01.2020 को सफलतापूर्वक किया गया।

इनको मुख्य विकास अधिकारी के पद का आवश्यक एवं प्रारम्भिक ज्ञान हो गया है। इस internship से ये जागरूक, प्रेरित और प्रोत्साहित हुये हैं। जिला प्रशासन इनके उज्ज्वल भविष्य की कामना करता है कि ये अपने इच्छित पद को प्राप्त कर सकें।

21/01/20

दिनांक : 21.01.2020
स्थान : बाँदा, उ.प्र.

आई.ए.एस.
जिलाधिकारी

"एक दिन का अधिकारी"

प्रमाण पत्र

कार्यालय : जिलाधिकारी, बाँदा, उ.प्र.

बाँदा जिला प्रशासन द्वारा छात्रों के व्यक्तित्व विकास, छात्र को अधिकारी बनने के लिये प्रेरणा एवं प्रोत्साहन देने तथा योज्यता में वृद्धि के उद्देश्य से चलाये जा रहे नवाचार कार्यक्रम "एक दिन का अधिकारी" के अन्तर्गत श्री नरेन्द्र कुमार कक्षा बी.ए. III yr. विद्यालय राजकीय महाविद्यालय-पिपरहरी जि.-बाँदा के द्वारा जिलाधिकारी के पद हेतु आवेदन किया गया। निम्नानुसार अपेक्षित कार्यवाही पूर्ण की गयी -

1. पद से सम्बन्धित कार्यों / दायित्वों का अध्ययन किया गया और 06.09.2019 को लेख प्रस्तुत किया गया।
2. सम्बन्धित कार्यालय का भ्रमण एवं सभी कार्यों का अध्ययन कर 25.09.2019 को लेख प्रस्तुत किया गया।
3. सम्बन्धित अधिकारी के साथ एक दिवसीय भ्रमण कर उनके कार्यों / दायित्वों के निर्वहन से सम्बन्धित अपनी सोच विकसित की और 10.12.2019 को लेख प्रस्तुत किया गया।
4. प्रशिक्षण के उपरान्त अपने अनुभवों का प्रस्तुतिकरण समिति के समक्ष पी.पी.टी. के माध्यम से 21.01.2020 को सफलतापूर्वक किया गया।

इनको जिलाधिकारी के पद का आवश्यक एवं प्रारम्भिक ज्ञान हो गया है। इस internship से ये जागरूक, प्रेरित और प्रोत्साहित हुये हैं। जिला प्रशासन इनके उज्ज्वल भविष्य की कामना करता है कि ये अपने इच्छित पद को प्राप्त कर सकें।

21/01/20

दिनांक : 21.01.2020
स्थान : बाँदा, उ.प्र.

हीरा लाल आई.ए.एस.
जिलाधिकारी, बाँदा

It was coordinated by Shri Rakesh Kumar Jain, District Savings Officer and Shri Koshalendra Kumar, District Employment Officer.

Efforts were made to build a science park in Banda. 5.68 acres of land was given in Kanshi Ram Smriti Upvan Park. The government gave approval to build a science park. This was a historic achievement for Banda.

बुंदेलखंड के पहले साइंस पार्क को शासन की मंजूरी

सवा तीन करोड़ से बनेगा, नए साल से शुरू होगा काम

The meritorious students were taken to IIT Kanpur and National Sugar Institute, Kanpur by Science Club, Banda.

- With the aim of developing the process of self-learning, the children were given an opportunity to acquire knowledge in the country's famous technical educational institution so that the students who wanted to make careers (future) in this field could get a new direction.
- During the visit, they were taken to modern scientific laboratories, central library, classrooms, airstrip, etc., where students were exposed to major subjects like supercomputer, 3D technology, laser technology, nanotechnology, etc.
- A tour of sugar factory and other places was also undertaken.

❑

3.9

Farmers' Prosperity

India is an agricultural country. India has roots in villages. Farmers live in the village. Water, forest, and land are the main capital of the farmer. Without making the farmer rich, our country cannot become a developed country.

We all have a dream that India should become a developed country very soon. To fulfil this objective, we need to make the farmer prosperous. Therefore, the Government of India has launched a plan to double the income of farmers in 2022–23 as compared to 2015–16.

The economy of Banda is agrarian. There is no industry here; whatever little industry is there is for the support of agriculture. The people of Banda have been doing farming for centuries. Farming is a loss-making activity particularly for small and marginal farmers. Therefore, it is very important to convert agriculture into business. Only then we can increase the income of the farmers. Farmer Producer Company (FPC) is being promoted in this direction. The farmers of the village will constitute and run the FPC together. They will convert farming into the agricultural business through this company. The main task is to change the thought process of farmers. You have to make them strong by giving them knowledge because knowledge is power. To change the thought process of the farmers and increase their power with new thought processes, many steps were taken, one after the other.

To increase the knowledge of different types of farming, farmers who were doing good work, and some of those who were doing better by adopting different methods of farming as well as those, who had more income than other farmers from agriculture and other sources were selected and sent on study tours.

- In today's scientific age, the need of the hour is to change the working style from time to time. People who do not incorporate new knowledge in their work process are left behind in society and are unable to make their mark at workplace, at home, etc. Keeping this fact in mind, the District Magistrate started 'Gyanarjan Yatras' for different groups like children, farmers, village heads, and small businessmen.
- This was done so that their knowledge could increase, their methodology could become systematic and they adopt modern technology and as well as carve out special identity for themselves in the society. Knowledge is power. The people of Banda can become powerful by acquiring knowledge in an atmosphere of joy and happiness.

समृद्धि किसान बाँदा का हो जाए इसलिए।
आय भी इसकी दोगुनी हो जाए इसलिए।
माहौल इस तरह का बनाया है डी.एम. ने।
खेती का सारा ज्ञान दिलाया है डी.एम. ने॥

—नज़रे आलम 'नज़र बाँदवी'

Objective

- Developing a procedure for doing comparative work.
- Familiarizing with modern technology and knowledge.
- To motivate different groups like children, farmers, village heads and businessmen, etc., to find knowledge and move forward using it as per time and requirement.

Process

- Selection of different target groups.
- Scheduling department-wise visits for selected target groups according to their work so that the department can facilitate their travel.
- Selection of major ideal/famous places for travel and preparation of reference material.

District level relevant nodal department for organizing visits

- **For children:** District Science Club, Banda
- **For farmers:** Agriculture Department, Horticulture Department, and Cooperative Department
- **For village heads:** Panchayati Raj Department
- **For milk producers:** Dairy Department

Tours for vegetable-growing farmers

Organized by Horticulture Department

With a view to increasing the income of the farmers of the district and connecting them to modern methods and learning by seeing, a three-day Gyanarjan Yatra was organized at the Centre of Excellence at Umarda, Kannauj. Its main objective was to make the farmers aware of the latest technology in vegetable cultivation and make vigorous efforts to increase their income by producing more vegetables in less time. It was led by Mr. Parvez Ahmed, the then district horticulture officer.

हरी झंडी दिखा किसानों को रवाना करते डीएम हीरालाल। अमर उजाला

सब्जी तकनीक सीखने कन्नौज गए 50 किसान

बांदा। जनपद के 50 प्रगतिशील किसान कन्नौज में सब्जी उत्पादन संबंधी प्रशिक्षण लेंगे। गुरुवार को जिलाधिकारी हीरा लाल ने हरी झंडी दिखाकर बस को रवाना किया। उन्होंने किसानों से कहा कि अभी की प्रगति और प्रशिक्षण के बाद की प्रगति का रोड मैप तैयार कर जिला प्रशासन को उपलब्ध कराएं। सब्जी उगाने की नई तकनीक सीखने के बाद अन्य किसानों को भी जागरुक करें। उद्यान अधिकारी परवेज खां को निर्देश दिए कि अगले सप्ताह महिलाओं को बाहर भेजने की कार्य योजना बनाएं। ब्यूरो

Women were sent on a tour under Integrated Horticulture Mission by the District Horticulture Department to Indian Vegetable Research Institute, Banaras. They brought modern knowledge. This knowledge proved effective in increasing their income.

वाराणसी में सीख रहीं सब्जी की खेती के गुर

Ideal village tour by Panchayati Department

What is an ideal village like? What facilities should it have for the public? How can the village heads play their role better in rural development? For this, the model village Knowledge Acquisition Tour was organized for the village heads to Pawa village panchayat of Lalitpur district and Itaura village panchayat of Jalaun district. This work was done under the supervision of Mr. Sanjay Kumar Yadav, district panchayat raj officer.

Under this program, schools with modern facilities, like child-friendly toilets, ponds, drinking water system, voice of Pawa, market places, waiting room, straw bank, village cleaning system, solar lights, secretariat, gym, NRLM group work, floriculture, roof water harvesting system Soakpit, ANM Centre and religious places, etc., were visited by the team.

Anna Hazare: With the inspiration of the District Magistrate, Banda, on 27 January 2020, under 'Gyanarjan Yatra' for the purpose of building a model village in Banda district, a delegation of village heads under the leadership of Mr. Muhammat Shafi, district adviser, (SBM-G) Panchayati Raj Department, was sent to Ralegan Siddhi and Hiware Bazar, the modern villages of Ahmednagar district of Maharashtra. Information about the work and operations undertaken there was obtained. The delegation also met eminent social worker Anna Hazareji in Ralegan Siddhi during the visit. During this visit, the delegation of the village heads also learnt about the profitable agriculture practices by the farmers along with the development of the village in view of the geographical situation. After returning from the tour, work was done in the village panchayats in Banda district, with the cooperation of the common people to develop the village panchayats, make them aware of cleanliness and conserve the depleting groundwater.

A study tour was organized for Gram Panchayat, Girwan, Chibaon, Jakhni, etc., development block Mahua, gram panchayat Benda, Sadidanpur of development block tindwari, Gram Panchayat Rampur, development block Jaspura, Gram Panchayat, Pista, Murwal, Mantha of development block Baberu village panchayat, Pannah, Chhilolar of Block Kamasin, Katra Kalinjar

Dhadwamanpur of development block Naraini, village Panchayat Bharehadu of development block Bisanda, gram panchayat Mahokhar Gureh of Para development block, Badekhar Khurd etc. The respective village heads of gram panchayats, who went on the study tour got inspired by it and made their major contribution in making their respective gram panchayats a model village. Other gram panchayats of the district also followed suit and took inspiration to make their gram panchayats a model. Shri Sankata Prasad Tripathi, President of the Union contributed a lot to this project.

रालेगांव सिद्धि से प्रेरणा लेकर संवारेंगे गांव

'Kisan Ki Baat Kisan Se' (Dialogue with farmer about farmer excursion tour by Agriculture Department

A group of 40 farmers from the district left for Daulatpur village, Barabanki district. They learnt and studied the progressive farm of Ram Sharan Vermaji, a respected progressive farmer of Daulatpur village and a Padma Shri awardee. The farmers were told about modern farming techniques and the nuances to be taken care of during production. Shri A. K. Singh, Deputy Director and Shri Pramod Kumar, District Agriculture Officer took interest and accomplished it.

Under the Horticulture Mission of the Horticulture Department, ₹1.08 crore was approved for Excellence Centre. It was proposed in the nursery of the Horticulture Department of Banda City.

Agriculture Department has a very big farm in Atarra tehsil. Under the National Agriculture Scheme, an Agriculture Excellence Centre of 2.85 crores was approved here so that along with Banda, all the information about agricultural crops could reach the entire Bundelkhand and farmers income would increase.

कृषि प्रक्षेत्र अतर्रा में लगे सोलर पंप का पानी देखते जिलाधिकारी।

कृषि प्रक्षेत्र कार्यालय के बाहर निरीक्षण करते जिलाधिकारी। • हिन्दुस्तान

माडल रूप में तैयार किया जाए अतर्रा कृषि प्रक्षेत्र

बांदा | हिन्दुस्तान संवाद

राजकीय कृषि एवं बीज सम्बर्धन प्रक्षेत्र अतर्रा का जिलाधिकारी ने निरीक्षण किया। तैयार की गई फसल को देखा और फसल सिंचाई के लिए स्थापित कराया गया सोलर पंप को भी देखा। कार्यालय में साफ सफाई और कृषि यंत्रों के रख रखाव सही से करने के निर्देश दिए। कृषि अधिकारी को निर्देश दिए कि कृषि फार्म हाउस को माडल के रुप में विकसित किया जाए। वन, पशु पालन, मत्स्य आदि विभागों के अधिकारियों को प्रक्षेत्र लाकर संचालित योजनाओं से प्रक्षेत्र का विकास कराया जाए।

बोले डीएम

- राजकीय कृषि फार्म हाउस का डीएम ने किया निरीक्षण
- फार्म को बेहतर बनाने के लिए अधिकारियों को दिए निर्देश

जिलाधिकारी हीरालाल ने कृषि फार्म हाउस अतर्रा का निरीक्षण किया। कहा कि इस फार्म को बहुउद्देशीय रुप में विकसित किया जाए। मत्स्य पालन विभाग के द्वारा तालाब व मत्स्य पालन करवाया जाए। पशु पालन विभाग के द्वारा पशु पालन कर जैविक खाद आदि तैयार कराई जाए। कृषि फार्म हाउस को माडल के रुप में विकसित करने के लिए कृषि निदेशक को पत्र लिखा जाए। कहा कि जो पेड़ सूख गए है वन विभाग से सम्पर्क कर कटवाकर वहां पर फलदार पौध रोपित कराए जाए। इसके बाद बीज गोदाम, भूसा गोदाम, जनरेटर व कृषि यंत्रों को देखा कहा कि कृषि यंत्रों का सही से रख रखाव किया जाए। कार्यालय की साफ सफाई नियमित कराई जाए। खराब कृषि यंत्रों की नीलामी कराई जाए। साथ ही नाली, खड़ंजा निर्माण के लिए प्रस्ताव तैयार करने के निर्देश दिए। कृषि फार्म हाउस में लगे सोलर पंप को देखा। इस मौके पर जिला कृषि अधिकारी प्रमोद कुमार, फार्म अधीक्षक लेखराज निरंजन आदि अधिकारी व कर्मचारी मौजूद रहे।

Kisan Mandi (Farmer Market Place) tour

Banda, Atarra and Baberu are the three farmers' marketplaces in Banda. In all three, ten farmers were respectfully invited every day by the marketing inspector and mandi assistant. Information was given about all the schemes of the Mandi (Market place) Department. After this, these farmers would visit the entire market complex and see all the activities. Accordingly, the farmers could get complete information and they took advantage of it. It was led by Ms. Vibha Khare, Secretary, Mandi.

An action plan was prepared to make clusters of agricultural product. Work was done to make clusters in the village where a particular crop was grown more in that village and in the surrounding villages. Emphasis was given on implementing all the rules and regulations of the cluster. A new idea arose from this. The benefits of the cluster began to accumulate. It proved helpful in increasing the income of farmers.

दैनिक जागरण, झाँसी, 29, नवम्बर

बाँदा : विकास भवन परिसर से किसानों को लखनऊ के लिये रवाना करते अधिकारीगण।

40 दुग्ध उत्पादक कृषकों को मिलेगा प्रशिक्षण

लखनऊ में बेहतर दुग्ध उत्पादन का हुनर सीखेंगे किसान

बाँदा ब्यूरो : खेती के साथ दुग्ध उत्पादन में किसानों का मुनाफा बढ़ाने के लिये उन्हें नई-नई तकनीकियों से दक्ष्य बनाया जायेगा। जनपद के 40 दुग्ध उत्पादक कृषक लखनऊ में दो दिन प्रशिक्षण लेंगे। कृषकों का दल विकास भवन से गुरूवार को लखनऊ के लिये रवाना हुआ। बुन्देलखण्ड का मुख्य व्यवसाय कृषि आधारित है। यहां खेती के साथ बड़ी संख्या में लोग दुग्ध उत्पादन व पशुपालन का काम करते हैं। खेती की तर्ज पर दुग्ध उत्पादन के कार्य को विकसित करने के लिये कृषकों को नई-नई तकनीकों से दक्ष बनाने का काम शुरू किया गया है। आत्मा योजना के अन्तर्गत गुरूवार को 40 किसान दुग्ध उत्पादन का प्रशिक्षण लेने के लिये लखनऊ रवाना हुये। विकास भवन परिसर में मुख्य विकास अधिकारी हरिश्चन्द्र वर्मा, उपकृषि निदेशक एके सिह व जिला कृषि अधिकारी डा० प्रमोद कुमार ने वाहनों को हरी झंडी दिखाकर किसानों के दल को रवाना किया। जिला कृषि अधिकारी ने बताया कि लखनऊ के चकगजरिया डेरी फार्म में कृषकों को दो दिवसीय प्रशिक्षण दिया जायेगा। जिसमें मुख्य रूप से यह जानकारी दी जायेगी कि जनपद व बुन्देलखण्ड के लिये पशुपालन में कौन से प्रजाति के पशु बेहतर हैं। दुग्ध के प्रोडक्टों के बारे में भी जानकारी दी जायेगी। ताकि किसान अपने दुग्ध से विभिन्न प्रकार के उत्पाद तैयार कर उनकी बिक्री कर सके। इसके अलावा आधुनिक तकनीकि के हुनर भी सिखाये जायेंगे। जिससे कि जनपद के पशुपालक व दुग्ध उत्पादन करने वाले कृषक उत्पादन की क्षमता बढ़ाकर अपने मुनाफे में बढ़ोतरी कर सके।

For milk producers: Dairy Department

Under the Dairy Development Programme, a budget of ₹103.16 crore was approved for setting up a dairy plant of one lakh litre per day capacity at the headquarters of Banda. It was for the entire Chitrakoot Mandal.

Vikas Bhawan tour

For the first time in the district, an innovative programme was launched with the aim of doubling the income of the farmers, which was named 'Kisan Vikas Tour'. In this programme, apart from Agriculture Department, all departmental information was given by other departments like Panchayati Raj Department, DRDA, Animal Husbandry Department and Agriculture Defence Section, NEDA Department, Social Welfare Department, Co-operative Department, and ICDS Department.

Objective

- To reduce the gap between government departments and farmers.

- To remove the hesitation from the minds of the farmers to meet officials through an important innovative programme and to empower the farmers by giving all the departmental information.

Process

- The following criteria were given priority in the selection of farmers by the field staff:
  1. Farmers who are educated.
  2. Those who have communication skills to convey their point of view to others.
  3. Those who have the eagerness, urge and willingness for learning.
  4. Those who have the desire to serve society and have social thinking.
- Bringing 10 farmers from each village panchayats to Vikas Bhawan through field staff and farmer assistants, ATM/ BTM, telling them about the development plans of all the departments and giving them all the leaflets, etc., available in the department.
- Promoting the use of the latest farming techniques, hybrid seeds, growing pulses and oilseeds in a scientific manner to commercialise the farming system with a view to doubling the income of the farmers.
- Information was provided about using quality certified seeds, getting more yield at less cost in farming, packaging and grading to get the right price for agricultural produce.
- Simultaneously involving fisheries, horticulture, milch animals, poultry and goat rearing, integrating all in the changing farming environment.
- Farmers were made aware so that they would try to move forward.

Result

Under this programme, from 25 December 2018 to 29 July 2019, a total of 1,083 farmers benefited by visiting Krishi Vikas Bhawan and other departments.

किसानों को विभागों का कराया गया भ्रमण, दी जानकारी

बांदा। जिले के विभिन्न न्याय पंचायत के अंतर्गत गांव के किसानों को विभागों का भ्रमण कराया जा रहा है। सोमवार को न्याय पंचायत खप्टिहाकला के विभिन्न गांव के करीब एक दर्जन किसानों को विकास भवन के विभिन्न विभागों का भ्रमण कराया गया। कार्यालयों में मौजूद अधिकारियों ने संचालित योजनाओं की जानकारी दी। किसानों ने अधिकारियों से भी योजनाओं के बारे में पूछा।

जिलाधिकारी के निर्देशन पर किसानों को विभिन्न विभागों का भ्रमण कराया जा रहा है। सोमवार को तिन्दवारी विकास खण्ड के न्याय पंचायत खप्टिहाकला के विभिन्न गांव के किसानों को सरकारी कार्यालयों का भ्रमण कराया गया। विकास भवन में मुख्य विकास अधिकारी कार्यालय में पहुंचकर किसानों ने जानकारी ली। सीडीओ हरिश्चन्द्र वर्मा ने किसानों को बताया कि खरीफ फसल का समय चल रहा है। कम लागत और अधिक पैदावार वाली फसलों को खेतों में तैयार करें।

इसके बाद जिला कृषि अधिकारी कार्यालय किसान पहुंचे। जहां पर जिला कृषि अधिकारी डा. प्रमोद कुमार ने किसानों को बताया कि कम सिंचाई वाली फसलों को तैयार करें। दलहन और तिलहन क्षेत्र में अधिक पैदावार होती है तो ऐसे में इन्हीं फसलों का चयन करें। साथ ही किसानों को सुझाव दिया कि कम बारिश और कीट रोगों सहित अन्य आपदा से फसल प्रभावित होने पर फसलों का बीमा जरूर कराए। प्रधानमंत्री फसल बीमा के तहत ब्लाक और तहसील स्तर पर बीमा कम्पनी के कर्मचारी नियुक्त किए गए है। कहा कि अपने खेतों में एक फसल की बुआई न करें जरुरत और पैदावार को देखते हुए कई फसलें अलग अलग खेतों में तैयार करें।

Arahar (Pigeon Pea) Conference

Branding of local agricultural products through Arahar (Pigeon Pea) Conference.

There is a good production of oilseeds, pulses, gram, mustard, etc., in Banda and entire Bundelkhand. Due to the scarcity of water, chemical fertilizers are not used much. This makes these products nutritious, delicious and organic. But people do not know about these products and benefits, due to which they are not much in demand. Due to less demand, the crop does not command a

good price. On 10 February 2020, on the occasion of World Oilseeds Day, a grand event of the Arahar Conference was organized in the midst of the arahar fields. After this conference, the visitors also visited the world-famous Kalinjar Fort. This also led to agricultural tourism. Five Padma Shri awardees who received awards for agricultural work participated in this conference. Shri Babulal Dahiya, Satna, Madhya Pradesh; Ram Sharan Verma, Barabanki, Uttar Pradesh; Kisan Chachi, Muzaffarpur, Bihar; Kanwal Singh Chauhan, Sonipat, Haryana; Bharat Bhushan Tyagi Padma Shri, Bulandshahr, Uttar Pradesh participated in it. Leading farmers from about 35 districts participated. They were given citations. Agents and traders from all 19 mandis in Bundelkhand were invited. Many scientists were invited. MP Shri R. K. Singh Patel and MLA Shri Rajkaran Kabir also participated. It was a unique method of publicity that was liked by the people. It was widely publicised. The next day all the major newspapers wrote a page about it. It impressed the people a lot.

Development of villages situated on the banks of rivers

Three rivers pass through Banda, namely Baghein, Yamuna and Ken. About 130 villages are situated on their banks. If Lucknow is situated on the banks of the Gomti River, Kanpur situated on the banks of Ganges river and Prayagraj situated on Sangam can be developed, then why can't these villages be developed? Efforts have been made in this direction. A public awareness meeting was organised by sending officers to all the villages which was called *'Aalao Pe Vikas Ka Choupal'* in winter. The developmental activity was started in these villages. These villages were shown the dream of development like Lucknow, Kanpur and Prayagraj, due to their being on the river banks. Letters were written to many organisations working in this area, asking for their cooperation.

नदी किनारे के 130 गांव बनेंगे मॉडल

हर अधिकारी एक गांव गोद लेकर करे तैयारी, अच्छे एनजीओ होंगे चिह्नित

अमर उजाला ब्यूरो

बांदा। नदी किनारे आबाद जिले के 130 गांवों को चार माह के अंदर मॉडल के रूप में विकसित करना है। इसके लिए हर अधिकारी एक-एक गांव गोद लेकर मंथन करें और योजना बनाएं। साथ ही पानी पर अच्छा काम कर रहे एनजीओ और कम से कम 10 सोशल लीडर भी तलाश करें।

यह बात डीएम हीरालाल ने अपने आवास पर फूलों के बीच आयोजित खिचड़ी चौपाल में अधिकारियों से कही। धरती पर बैठकर दोना पत्तल में खिचड़ी और मिट्टी के कुल्हड़ में पानी लिया। ये सब वही अधिकारी हैं, जिन्होंने नदी किनारे आबाद गांवों में खिचड़ी भोज और चौपालों का आयोजन कर ग्रामीणों को नदी प्रदूषित न करने की प्रेरणा दी। अफसरों से कहा कि अच्छी सोच के साथ अपनी जिम्मेदारियों का निर्वहन करें। कहा कि इसी सोच के साथ नदी किनारे आबाद 130 गांवों को तीन से चार माह में मॉडल के रूप में तैयार करना है। नदियों की अहमियत बताई। एडीएम संतोष बहादुर सिंह व संजय कुमार, सीडीओ हरिश्चंद्र वर्मा, पीडी आरपी मिश्रा, सिटी मजिस्ट्रेट सुरेश कुमार, कृषि उप निदेशक एके सिंह, बीएसए हरिश्चंद्रनाथ, एसडीएम नैनी वंदिता श्रीवास्तव, मुख्य पशु चिकित्साधिकारी डा. आईएन सिंह, उद्यान अधिकारी परवेज अधिकारी, अर्थ एवं संख्याधिकारी संजीव बघेल, अपर सूचना अधिकारी कु. शारदा, रिटायर्ड, विशेष कार्याधिकारी मुहीब अहमद, रिटायर्ड एओ सईद अहमद, योगेश बाबू, प्रदीप गुप्ता भी मौजूद रहे।

चौपाल में खिचड़ी का भोज करते डीएम व अन्य अधिकारी। संवाद

❑

3.10

Plastic-free Banda

We all know that plastic does not decompose for thousands of years. Plastic is causing a threat to human life as well as the earth's atmosphere and causing climate change. Animals and birds are dying from eating plastic. Every year 10,00,000 marine lives in the ocean lose lives by eating plastic material. Along with this, plastic is polluting and destroying the fertility of the soil.

Cancer is caused by plastic bottles, utensils, etc. Plastic causes floods and destruction by creating blockages in rivers and streams. Keeping in view the disadvantages caused by the use of plastic, with the aim of making the district plastic-free from 19 August 2019, a campaign was started after preparing an action plan with citizens taking a pledge, which was given a slogan—*'Jhola-yukt, plastic-mukt, Banda'*.

बीमारियों से सबको बचाएगी यह मुहिम।
वातावरण को स्वच्छ बनाएगी यह मुहिम।
डी.एम. की है अपील कि जुड़ जाइए सभी।
पन्नी को छोड़ झोले से जुड़ जाइए सभी॥

—नज़रे आलम नज़र' बाँदवी'

Objective

- To make efforts to reduce plastic pollution in the district.
- To create a clean environment.
- Try to prevent pollution-borne diseases.
- To make people aware to decrease the plastic industry gradually.

Process

- Meetings were held with officials and businessmen.
- Public awareness programs were organized.
- Cloth bags were distributed to the public, motivating the general public to use cloth bags as an alternative to plastic.

  A message was circulated that if anyone was found with the banned plastic, then punitive action would be taken against them.

अब झोला युक्त, प्लास्टिक मुक्त होगा बांदा

कैंसर से बचने के लिये पॉलिथीन का बन्द करें प्रयोग : डीएम

कपड़े के थैलों से लैस नजर आएंगे अधिकारी व कर्मचारी

आदेश

- The traders, educational institutions and the public in the district were administered a pledge not to use plastic in their daily lives.

- Cloth bags were distributed among the commercial establishments and the public by the district magistrate after collecting the pledges.

Result

- The efforts of the District Magistrate had a profound effect on the traders and public.
- Merchants started delivering goods in biodegradable bags.
- The public was seen to be making a successful attempt to use cloth bags in their daily life.
- Simultaneously, to make the campaign stronger, the use of copper/steel/earthenware was encouraged to stop the use of plastic bottles.
- Emphasis was laid on the use of earthenware in the district. Officers and employees started using it.
- This effort will continue till the district becomes completely plastic-free.

Earthenware: First, an order was issued asking that tea should be served in *kulhads* in the meetings. It is healthy and is good for the environment. To promote earthenware for eating and

कुम्हारों को डीएम की सौगा

drinking, an earthenware trader was invited, and an exhibition was organized in Sadar tehsil. For the availability of earthenware in the city, an earthenware shop was opened. I personally inaugurated it. In the district magistrate's bungalow, all the utensils were made of earthenware. All the potters in the district were called and felicitated and encouraged. On Diwali, the Deputy Collector and I personally went to their homes and offered sweets to boost their morale. I reviewed the pottery art lease. The removal of plastic and increasing the use of earthenware were a part of the campaign.

Plates and bowls made of leaves: Efforts were made to increase the circulation of plates and bowls made of leaves for eating and drinking. I went to the shop of two sellers on the sidewalk and saw and understood their work. During meetings, I would eat sitting on the floor from the plates and bowls made of leaves so that people would get inspired and make it a habit.

दोना-पत्तल बेचने वाले सम्मानित

फुटपाथी दुकानदारों को डीएम हीरालाल ने माला पहनाकर मिठाई दी

अमर उजाला ब्यूरो

बांदा। महंगे और चमकते-दमकते शोरूम में सजी क्राकरी और प्लास्टिक, पॉलिथीन और थर्माकोल के बर्तनों से रुझान हटाकर दोना-पत्तल के रीति और रिवाज को फिर जीवित करने के लिए चलाए जा रहे अभियान में डीएम हीरालाल ने गुरुवार को शहर में फुटपाथों पर दोना-पत्तल बेच रहे गरीब दुकानदारों से मुलाकात की। उन्हें माला पहनाकर सम्मानित किया और मिठाई का डिब्बा सौंपा। दोना-पत्तल को और बढ़ावा देने पर जोर दिया। शहर कोतवाली के आसपास फुटपाथों पर रोजाना महिला-पुरुष दोना-पत्तल बेचते हैं। इन्हीं में से कल्लू, अशोक, बेबी और कृष्णा आदि से डीएम मिले और उन्हें प्रोत्साहित किया। उनकी समस्याएं पूछीं। बांदा के बाशिंदों से कहा कि समारोहों में दोना-पत्तल और कुल्हड़ के इस्तेमाल का पुराना रिवाज फिर वापस ले आएं तो पर्यावरण में काफी सुधार आएगा। डीएम ने कहा कि ऐसे समारोहों में वह खुद शामिल होंगे और वह पौधों का वितरण भी करेंगे। डीएम ने अपने साथ मौजूद सिटी मजिस्ट्रेट सुरेंद्र सिंह को निर्देश दिया कि प्लास्टिक हटाओ अभियान में तेजी लाएं। साथ ही दोना-पत्तल और माटी कला के व्यवसायियों को चिन्हित कर उनकी समस्याओं का समाधान करें और उनके व्यवसाय में यथासंभव मदद करें। साथ ही मौके पर मौजूद तहसीलदार अवधेश कुमार निगम को कहा कि दोना-पत्तल और कुल्हड़ के प्रति लोगों का रुझान बढ़ाने के लिए कार्यक्रम तैयार करें। सिटी मजिस्ट्रेट के स्टेनो मोहम्मद अशरफ और डीएम कैंप कार्यालय के सलमान आदि भी थे।

दोना-पत्तल बेचने वालों के साथ डीएम हीरा लाल, सिटी मजिस्ट्रेट।

❑

3.11

The Wall of Kindness

One day, Mr. Avashesh Kumar Nigam, tehsildar, Sadar Banda, told me that a program named the 'Wall of Kindness' was being run by him. I went to the location and observed it closely. Many poor people were being helped by this program. This program saw good use of the items that were no more of use to us. This important aspect impressed me. On the spot, I decided that it would be implemented in the five tehsils of the district under the leadership of Mr. Nigam.

After returning from the location, I did research on it and found that this program was being implemented in some other cities, too. This virtuous work of Nigamji was started in Banda and I liked it very much. Within a month, the Wall of Kindness started in Atarra, Naraini, Baberu and Pailani, too.

इनसानियत का जज्बा जगाने के वास्ते।
इनसान को इनसान बनाने के वास्ते।
नेकी की एक दीवार सजाई गई है यूँ।
कितने घरों की लाज बचाई गई है यूँ॥

—नज़रे आलम 'नज़र बाँदवी'

Objective

- Discharging our responsibilities towards society.

- To develop the spirit of becoming and creating responsible citizens.
- To develop generosity and charitable attitude in the citizens.
- To motivate the society to cooperate for the weaker sections.
- Proper management of unnecessary/unusable items.
- To develop a sense of satisfaction in one's personality.
- Creating a positive identity in the family, and society.
- To provide a meaningful platform between charitable people and the needy.
- To develop the spirit of helping each other in society.
- To provide a platform to the spirit of social service within every person and to awaken this spirit.

दैनिक जागरण, झाँसी, 15, सितम्बर

तहसीलदार की पहल से बनी तहसील परिसर में नेकी की दीवार

अन्य विभाग संचालित करेंगे नेकी की दीवार : डीएम

बाँदा ब्यूरो : जिलाधिकारी ने सदर तहसील में नेकी की दीवार मुहिम के तहत सहयोग करने वाले तहसीलदार समेत लेखपाल अमीन व लिपिक आदि कर्मचारियों को प्रशस्ति पत्र प्रदान कर उन्हें सम्मानित किया। अनेक अधिकारियों ने अपने विभाग में नेकी की दीवार संचालित करने का संकल्प लिया।

उल्लेखनीय है कि जिलाधिकारी हीरा लाल द्वारा सदर तहसील में पिछली 25 अगस्त से संचालित नेकी की दीवार पर टंगे वस्त्रों का अवलोकन किया और प्रसन्नता जताई कि यह सामग्री गरीबों के हितों में काम आएगी। इस दौरान नगर मजिस्ट्रेट, मेडिकल कालेज प्राचार्य, बेसिक शिक्षाधिकारी, जेलर, महिला कालेज के प्रोफेसर, वन विभाग, स्वास्थ्य, विकास समेत जनपद स्तरीय अनेक अधिकारियों ने अपने-अपने विभागों में नेकी की दीवार संचालित करने का संकल्प लिया।

बाँदा : तहसील में नेकी की दीवार कार्यक्रम में प्रमाण पत्र देते डीएम।

Process

- Selecting the wall at any public place, office or establishment.
- To select 2–3 government employees dedicated to the noble cause to work as volunteers.
- To paint the Wall of Kindness in a colour different from the colour of the building.
- 'With the cooperation of all of you, to the cooperation of all of you' should be inscribed on the Wall of Kindness.

- You can leave all your spare/unusable clothing/ accessories here.
- The needy can take the items of their need/use from here free of cost.
- To monitor the above from anti-social elements, either a CCTV camera can be installed near the wall, or a person can be appointed for surveillance.
- A room should be converted into a storage room to keep clothes/shoes, slippers, notebooks/books and other household items provided by the donors.
- While receiving the above items from the donors, care has to be taken that the clothes are not torn/dirty, etc., and other materials (food, etc.,) are suitable for use.
- In a register of donors, full details like name, address, designation, mobile number, etc., will be recorded.
- The person receiving the goods/clothes for the 'Wall of Kindness' will be monitored, but his self-respect will be maintained and information about his name, address, etc., should not be taken from him.
- Kind-hearted citizens with charitable tendencies should be felicitated from time to time so that more and more people become a source of inspiration for the society.
- Establishments/offices/social workers operating the 'Wall of Kindness' will be felicitated by the district magistrate, Banda from time to time.

Result

- Helpless, needy and poor people in the district take their goods free of cost from the 'Wall of Kindness', which helps the people of this segment.

- The people who cooperate for the 'Wall of Kindness' get an opportunity to do social service.

'नेकी की दीवार' में सहयोग करने वालों को मिला प्रशस्ति पत्र

■ सहारा न्यूज ब्यूरो

बांदा।

तहसील सदर में बीते 25 अगस्त से संचालित नेकी की दीवार का निरीक्षण जिलाधिकारी द्वारा शुक्रवार को किया गया। जिसमें उन्होंने इस पुनीत कार्य की सराहना की। उन्होंने कहा कि लोगों के घरों में अतिरिक्त पड़ी सामग्री का जरूरतमंद लोगों के उपयोग में आ जाती है। इससे प्रेरित होकर चारो तहसीलों के एसडीएम ने अपनी अपनी तहसीलों में नेकी की दीवार की मुहिम चलाने का संकल्प लिया। शनिवार को जिलाधिकारी ने नेकी की दीवार में सहयोग करने वालों को प्रशस्ति पत्र देकर सम्मानित किया।

शनिवार को दोपहर एक बजे जिलाधिकारी हीरालाल ने नेकी की दीवार मुहिम के अन्तर्गत सहयोग करने वाले अवधेश कुमार निगम तहसीलदार बांदा, रमेश कुमार श्रीवास्तव लेखपाल, रमेश चन्द्र अवस्थी लेखपाल, सुरेश कुमार श्रीवास्तव लेखपाल, रामकृष्ण त्रिपाठी संग्रह अमीन, सुशील कुमार नजारत चतुर्थ श्रेणी, दिनेश कुमार राजस्व लिपिक, कमलेश बाबू लेखपाल, रामकिशोर वर्मा लेखपाल, संतोष देवी चतुर्थ श्रेणी नजारत, अब्दुल मजीद लेखपाल, अमरदीप गौतम लेखपाल, कुमारी प्रीती कुशवाहा लेखपाल, फूलचन्द्र पाण्डेय राजस्व निरीक्षक आफिस को सम्मानित करते हुये प्रशस्ति पत्र प्रदान किया गया। इस मुहिम के अन्तर्गत कानसेप्ट नोट का वितरण किया गया। जिसमें इसके उद्देश्य एवं प्रक्रिया का विस्तृत उल्लेख किया गया है।

बांदा : नेकी की दीवार में सहयोग करने वाले लोग प्रमाण पत्रों के साथ, साथ में हैं जिलाधिकारी हीरालाल। फोटो : एसएनबी

शुक्रवार को जिलाधिकारी ने किया था नेकी की दीवार का निरीक्षण

चारो एसडीएम ने अपनी तहसीलों में संचालित करने का लिया संकल्प

इस अवसर पर नगर मजिस्ट्रेट, प्राचार्य राजकीय मेडिकल कालेज बांदा, जिला बेसिक शिक्षा अधिकारी, जेलर, राजकीय महिला डिग्री कालेज के प्रोफेसर, वन विभाग, स्वास्थ्य विभाग व विकास विभाग के जनपद स्तरीय अधिकारी उपस्थित रहे। इनके द्वारा अपने अपने विभागों में नेकी की दीवार संचालित करने का संकल्प लिया गया।

❑

3.12

Banda Tourism

Tourism is a social, cultural, and economic activity. In this journey, the general public gets out of their everyday environment and goes to a tourist place. There are mainly four types of tourism:

1. International tourism
2. State tourism
3. Long-distance tourism
4. Short-distance tourism

Banda is historically, culturally, and geographically a district with great potential and opportunity for tourism development. Converting this potential into reality is a challenge. Tourism increases the income of the people and provides new employment opportunities to the common man and it creates new, attractive and enjoyable places for entertainment.

The people of Banda used to complaint that there were no attractions in Banda. That is what drew my attention to tourism. I started developing various places in Banda as tourist destinations to increase economic and employment development.

Kalinjar Fort: Kalinjar Development Committee was formed under the chairmanship of the district magistrate for its development.

- This historical Kalinjar Fort, protected by the government of India, and located in Banda district of Uttar Pradesh, is a unique work of world heritage. This fort is counted among the eight main forts of the Chandels.
- Situated on the border of Uttar Pradesh and Madhya Pradesh, this fort has been playing an important role as a vigilant overseer since time immemorial.
- Here Kalinjar and Shiva are complementary and synonymous with each other. In the inscriptions, it is mentioned as Kalinjar, Kalinjaradri, Kalinjargiri, Kalinjarpur, etc., the abode of Shiva (Neelkanth).
- The mythological significance of Kalinjar is related to Shiva drinking the poison which turned his throat, blue.

Prominent places to visit

On the north, the fort has seven gates named Alamgir Darwaza, Ganesh Darwaza, Chauburji Darwaza, Buddha Bhadra Darwaza, Hanuman Dwar, Lal Darwaza and Bara Darwaza.

- There are magnificent palaces called Raja Mahal and Rani Mahal.
- Sita Sej and Sitakund, monuments made of stone.
- Two combined ponds named Budha-Budhiya, which are beneficial for skin diseases.
- Where thousands of pilgrims visit Koti Teerth.
- Statue of Manduk Bhairav and Bhairavi made by digging the rock at an inaccessible place.
- Patal Ganga, Pandav Kund, Siddha's Cave, Bhairav Kund, Ramkatora Tal, Surasari Ganga, Bal Khandeshwar, Charan Paduka, Bhadyanchar, etc., are places of interest.
- Huge Kalpavriksha.

- The legendary Neelkanth temple.
- Steep ranges for rock climbing.

माहौल हो रहा है बड़ा खुशगवार भी,
पर्यटन से बढ़ रहा है यहाँ रोजगार भी।
डी.एम. ने पर्यटन की तरफ ध्यान दे दिया,
सेहत का और सुकून का सामान दे दिया।

—नज़रे आलम 'नज़र बाँदवी'

Arahar convention was held at the foothills below Kalinjar. Agricultural tourism was promoted. A huge plantation was carried out all around the fort so that the greenery would increase. A four-day Kalinjar Mahotsav was organized from 20 to 23 February 2020. The event was successfully concluded in an attractive manner under the leadership of Ms. Vandita Srivastava, Deputy Collector, Naraini.

दर्शकों को भाया अनुष्का का काली नृत्य

कालिंजर दुर्ग को अंतर्राष्ट्रीय पर्यटन स्थल बनाने की कवायद हुई तेज

विकास समिति की बैठक में डीएम ने दिए निर्देश, केंद्र सरकार ने स्वीकृत किए 8 करोड़ रुपये

Bhuragarh Fort

Bhuragarh Fort is situated on the banks of the Ken River, adjacent to the city of Banda. The history and importance of the fort are associated with the reign of the Bundelas, the sons of Maharaja Chhatrasal. The history of many revolutionaries is associated with this fort. This fort is a symbol of sacrifice, patriotism, sovereignty and equality.

A fair is held in Bhuragarh Fort, five days before Makar Sankranti. This fair is called the 'Fair of Lovers'. To find their love, people come here to worship and make a wish. By doing this in the temple of Natbaba located under the fort, they find their desired partner—this is the belief of the people here. It is the story of Natbaba related to love that attracts people to do so. This is a conserved fort.

नटबली में आज से शुरू होगा 2 दिवसीय मेला

शान्ति व सुरक्षा व्यवस्था के लिये तैनात किये गये मैजिस्ट्रेट

बाँदा ब्यूरो। केन नदी तट पर ऐतिहासिक भूरागढ़ दुर्ग में नटबली की समाधि पर दो दिवसीय मेले की शुरूआत 14 जनवरी को होगी। इस सम्बन्ध में बैठक के दौरान जिला प्रशासन द्वारा तैयारियों को अन्तिम रूप दिया गया। शान्ति एवं सुरक्षा व्यवस्था के लिये मैजिस्ट्रेट तैनात किये गये है। ऐतिहासिक दुर्ग भूरागढ़ एवं नटबली समाधि पर 14 व 15 जनवरी को विशाल मेला लगता है। जिसमें शहर व आसपास के गाँवों से लोग बड़ी संख्या में पहुँचते है। विकासभवन सभागार में मुख्य विकास अधिकारी हरिश्चन्द्र वर्मा की अध्यक्षता में बैठक आयोजित हुई। सीडीओ ने बताया कि जिलाधिकारी द्वारा मेले की तैयारियों को समय से पूर्ण करने के निर्देश दिये गये है। उन्होंने कहा कि मेले के दौरान केन नदी घाटी पर बड़ी संख्या में श्रद्धालु स्नान करते है। लिहाजा पर्याप्त संख्या में पुलिस बल तैनाती के लिये पुलिस अधीक्षक से अनुरोध किया गया। शान्ति एवं सुरक्षा व्यवस्था के लिये मैजिस्ट्रेट नामित किये गये। नगर मैजिस्ट्रेट को मेला मैजिस्ट्रेट के रूप में जिम्मेदारी दी गई है। बाँदा-झाँसी राजमार्ग पर जाम की स्थिति से निपटने के लिये प्रभारी अधिकारी यातायात वहीं रेल पटरी व केन नदी के रेलवे पुल पर सुरक्षा व्यवस्था का जिम्मा प्रभारी निरीक्षक रेलवे पुलिस तथा जीआरपी के जवान सम्भालेंगे। मेले के दौरान रेल संचालन के लिये रेल चालकों को हॉर्न देते हुये संचालन के दौरान हॉर्न बजाने के लिये स्टेशन मास्टर से अपेक्षा की गई। पावर कार्पोरेशन ग्रामीण एवं पेयजल से सम्बन्धित विभाग के अधिशासी अभियंताओं को निर्देश दिये गये कि विद्युत लाइनों का परीक्षण एवं आवश्यकतानुसार मरम्मत कराकर निर्बाध गति से विद्युत आपूर्ति की जाये। जल संस्थान को टैंकरों से पेयजल आपूर्ति के लिये निर्देशित किया गया। नगर पालिका ईओ,जिला पंचायत राज अधिकारी तथा बड़ोखर के खण्ड विकास अधिकारी को सफाई व्यवस्था के निर्देश दिये गये। बताते चलें कि मेले में व्यवस्थाओं को लेकर मेला समिति की ओर से मदन मोहन शर्मा मानव ने जिलाधिकारी को पत्र लिखा था। जिसके क्रम में प्रशासन द्वारा तैयारियों को पूर्ण किया गया। बैठक में सम्बन्धित विभागों के अधिकारी मौजूद रहे।

सीडीओ हरिश्चन्द्र वर्मा।

बाँदा- ऐतिहासिक नटबली मेले के लिए सफाई के बाद तैयार मन्दिर।

डीएम आज वितरित करेंगे पौध

बाँदा। केन नदी तट पर ऐतिहासिक भूरागढ़ दुर्ग के पास नटबली समाधि में लगने वाले मेले के पहले दिन 14 जनवरी को जिलाधिकारी हीरा लाल लोगों को पर्यावरण संरक्षण के प्रति जागरूक करेंगे। मण्डी परिसर में दोपहर 12 बजे से 2 बजे तक जिलाधिकारी द्वारा फलदार पौधों का वितरण किया जायेगा। पौध वितरण समारोह के दौरान सीडीओ हरिश्चन्द्र वर्मा,जिला उद्यान अधिकारी परवेज खां सहित सम्बन्धित विभागों के अधिकारी उपस्थित रहेंगे। वहीं अखिल भारतीय उद्योग व्यापार मण्डल के जिलाध्यक्ष मनोज जैन,पूर्व चेयरमैन राजकुमार राज,अमित सेठ भोलू,रजत सेठ,नटबली समाधि मन्दिर में भव्य कलश की स्थापना करायेंगे। साथ ही मुख्य विकास अधिकारी के स्टेनो अनूप रावत एवं महमूद हुसैन उर्फ बिल्ला भईया द्वारा गत वर्षों की भाँति 14 जनवरी को सुबह 9 बजे नटबली मन्दिर परिसर में खिचड़ी भोज का आयोजन किया जायेगा। श्री रावत ने अधिक से अधिक लोगों से खिचड़ी भोज में शामिल होकर प्रसाद ग्रहण करने की अपील की।

Bambeshwar Hill

- This mountain, adjacent to the city of Banda and the Ken River, is the highest mountain in the area. From here, one gets a panoramic and scenic view of entire Banda. The beautiful colours of sunrise can be seen from here.
- A plan to develop Bambeshwar Mountain as a Surya Darshan Sthal was prepared and developed.

ांबेश्वर पहाड़ पर बनेगा सूर्य दर्शन स्थ

र पहाड़ का अफसरों के साथ निरीक्षण करते डीएम हीरालाल। अमर उजाला

उजाला ब्यूरो

शहर के बांबेश्वर पहाड़ को र्शन स्थल के रूप में विकसित जाएगा, ताकि लोग तड़के यहां दर्शन कर सकें। साथ ही प्वाइंट भी बनेगा। संबंधित को इसकी कार्य योजना तैयार के निर्देश डीएम हीरालाल ने दिए हैं।

सोमवार को तड़के डीएम बांबेश्वर पहाड़ पहुंच गए। दुर्गम रास्तों और चट्टानों को पार कर पहाड़ की चोटी पर बैठकर पूरा जायजा लिया। शहर का विहंगम दृश्य दर्शनीय था। उसी समय सूर्योदय हो रहा था। पहाड़ से यह नजारा बेहद लुभावना था। अपने साथ मौजूद अधिकारियों और खासकर नगर पालिका ईओ संतोष कुमार मिश्रा और जल संस्थान अधिकारियों को निर्देश दिए कि पहाड़ की चोटी पर स्थित मंदिर तक जाने के लिए शेष सीढ़ियों का भी निर्माण कराएं। इस स्थान पर सूर्य दर्शन स्थल और सेल्फी प्वाइंट विकसित कराएं। नगर पालिका ईओ को रास्ते की सफाई और स लाइट के निर्देश दिए। कहा कि लागत पर इस स्थान को आ पर्यटन स्थल के रूप में विक किया जा सकता है। एसडी सुरजीत सिंह, अर्थ एवं संख्याधि संजीव बघेल, आरईएस एक्स शमीम अहमद, तहसीलदार अ निगम भी शामिल रहे।

गोशालाओं का आकस्मिक निरीक्षण

सिंधवारी। डीएम हीरालाल ने सोमवार की दोपहर यहां स्थित कान्हा आश्रय केंद्र का निरीक्षण किया। गोबर बायो गैस प्लांट सहित अन्य व्यवस्थाएं एक हफ्ते में दुरुस्त करने के निर्देश दिए। डीएम को यहां 206 पशु नजर आए। सभी में टैग लगे थे। इसके अलावा कस्बे में भी कई अन्ना पशु घूमते दिख पड़े। डीएम ने उन्हें तत्काल गोशाला लाने के निर्देश दिए। खाली पड़े मैदान में टिनशेड और पौधरोपण के लिए नगर पंचायत ईओ अजय कुमार यादव को निर्देश दिए। निरीक्षण के समय एसडीएम सुरजीत सिंह, पशु चिकित्साधिकारी नंदलाल कुशवाहा, चेयरमैन प्रतिनिधि भूरेलाल फौजी, सि राजनारायण सिंह सहित राजस्व विभाग के कर्मी उपस्थित रहे। डीएम ने इसके बाद गोआश्रय स्थल, खप्टिहा कला, जय हनुमान गो सेवा समिति, पिपरहरी, गो सेवा केंद्र, तुर्रा एवं गौतम पुरवा का भी निरीक्षण किया। मुख्य पशु चिकित्साधिकारी डा. आईएन सिंह को निर्देश दिए कि गोशाला के पशु का सत्यापन कराएं। फर्जी आंकड़े पाए गए तो सख्त कार्रवाई की जाएगी। एसडीएम, पैलानी मंसूर अहमद, एसडीएम अतर्रा सौरभ शुक्ला आदि भी उपस्थित रहे।

Ken Selfie Point and Ken Aarti

Selfie point was built on the banks of Ken which is the main river here. Jal Aarti on the Ken is performed every Tuesday from 26 November 2019, to make the public aware of the lifeline of Banda—the Ken River, and water conservation. Along with this, Jal Aarti is also performed at other rivers of the district like

Bagein, Yamuna, etc. It was organized by municipal executive officer and Assistant Engineer, Mr Shreesh Singh.

अब केन नदी में भी होगी जल आरती

डीएम हीरालाल बोले-सुबह-शाम सैर सपाटे की होगी व्यवस्था, सेल्फी प्वाइंट भी बनेगा

Under water conservation awareness campaign to honour the life-giver and lifeline of Banda—the Ken River, on 17 January 2020, Shri Raju Srivastava, Comedy King/Chairman, Film Development Council, Uttar Pradesh, through his comedy program administered the oath of water conservation to the general public while explaining the usage of water and warning about the future. It was coordinated by Saeed Ahmed, a retired administrative officer.

Oxygen Park

In Banda district, due to the lack of public entertainment places, the towns people were deprived of going out with their families for entertainment; the children did not have any open places to play. The Oxygen Park was developed so that the families could go out for walks in fresh air. Life is governed by a variety of systems. We build houses to live in. Wells, ponds, and taps are arranged for drinking water. Provision of electricity/solar is made for lighting. But we do not think about that with which we survive (24×7). Very few people understand the importance of the air we inhale when asleep or awake having made no effort to get oxygen (O_2). We get a free and unlimited amount of oxygen from the atmosphere. Due to urbanization, the density of population in cities is increasing, leading to a shortage of oxygen. The main reason behind this is that we do not make any meaningful effort for planting trees; rather, the amount of oxygen has decreased due to the continuous and indiscriminate felling of trees.

Cutting trees increases pollution. Due to the lack of oxygen in the atmosphere, various types of life-threatening diseases are increasing and life span is decreasing, whereas pure oxygen is needed in abundance for a healthy and happy life. For this, we should think about generating oxygen just like we generate electricity for homes. This is the very first important need of our life, which we do not fully understand. To achieve this objective, a new experiment is being conducted in the district.

जिले को जल्द मिलेगा ऑक्सीजन पार्क का तोहफा

नवाबटैंक के पास कई विभाग मिलकर बनाएंगे आकर्षक पार्क, डीएम ने निरीक्षण कर अधिकारियों को दिए जरूरी निर्देश।

किसानों को जल्द जारी होंगे 116 करोड़

The work was started by designing a project of construction of Chetna Park (area 0.368 hectares) of Forest Department located next to the famous Nawab Tank of Banda City and Forest Corporation Depot (area 1.12 hectares), Forest Department Nursery (Area 4.532 hectares) and a pond of the Irrigation Department and Sardar Vallabhbhai Patel Oxygen Park, in the land adjacent to the guest house of the department. Such plants were planted in it, so that they would generate oxygen. Due to this, oxygen would be available in abundance not only to the residents of the city, but also to the residents of the district.

With the help and coordination of Irrigation Department, Forest Corporation, Banda Development Authority, Sports Department and District Horticulture Department, meaningful efforts were made to develop this oxygen park on the lines of Ram Manohar Lohia Park and Janeshwar Mishra Park in Lucknow. Due to this, the people of Banda district got greenery and happiness along with oxygen. This project was led and coordinated by Shri Arvind Kumar Pandey, Executive Engineer, Ken Canal.

Irrigation Department has one park each in Atarra and Baberu tehsils, too. Their areas are 3.372 hectares and 1.878 hectares respectively. Both of them were also developed like this oxygen park so that this facility can be made available at tehsil level, too. It does not seem very attractive and effective to see and hear, but when the news is published calling Delhi a gas chamber due to Delhi's increased level of pollution and lack of oxygen, then we realise that we should make this effort in time. Such experiments should be carried out in every district so that pure oxygen can flow from different districts to the entire state and the environment can be prevented from getting polluted.

The Oxygen Park was developed around the Nawab Tank which had water. There is a natural and intrinsic relationship between water and forest. This site (water-forest) will increase the 'happiness index' of Banda. Efforts are on to develop Nawab Tank and Oxygen Park along with Kalinjar as tourist destinations.

Oxygen Park will make a big contribution to developing it as a tourism district.

Prof. Debashish Das Gupta, IIM Lucknow, gave us all the information and knowledge free of cost to prepare a concrete strategy for them. He came to Banda and visited all the locations and gave full support for developing the tourist spots.

Tourism Officer Shri Shakti Singh also gave impetus to it by reviewing several projects being implemented by the department for tourism development in the district. By holding meetings with hotel and travel associations, everyone's cooperation was obtained in promoting tourism.

❑

3.13

Women Development

Women constitute about half of our population. Without women's development, the dream of making the country a 'developed country' cannot be fulfilled. For women's development, it is most necessary that they should communicate, and cooperate with each other so that their strength increases. When all of them work together, there will be more profit with less cost and less time. With this view, self-help groups were formed. Various types of assistance were also given to these women groups. National Rural Livelihood Mission is engaged in this work. It is a holy act to bring women out of the walls of the house and make them come together. With the strength of the group, the goal is to develop all the women members in all respects.

A committee has been formed in each block under the chairmanship of the District Magistrate. It has a management office. It has 6 types of district mission managers. Similarly, each block has a Block Mission Management Office headed by a block development officer/project officer. In this, 7 types of block mission managers work. The mission of the country and the state directs the mission of the district.

Priority was given to women's development in Banda district and it was taken forward by focusing on a total of 6 activities:

1. Dairy development.
2. New source of income from the neem tree.
3. Bundelkhand Women Empowerment Broiler Rearing Scheme of Veterinary Department.
4. Trading related to gram, tur, jaggery, etc.
5. **Study Tour:** Deendayal Entrepreneurship Development Research Institute, Chitrakoot (Banda).
6. **Yoga:** So that women remain healthy and don't fall ill.

कमजोर को मजबूत बनाया है डी.एम. ने,
महिलाओं का सम्मान बढ़ाया है डी.एम. ने।
हर क्षेत्र में महिलाओं को अवसर दिला दिया,
महिलाओं को समाज में आगे बढ़ा दिया।

—नज़रे आलम 'नज़र बाँदवी'

बांदा में महिला समूहों के लिए पांच परियोजनाएं लागू

नीम की निबौली से आमदनी बढ़ाएंगी महिलाएं, अप्रैल से शुरु होगी खरीद, 15 रुपये किलो भाव,नीम-गुण उपयोग लाभ संगोष्ठी में नीम पर चर्चा

डीएम नीम रत्न से सम्मानित

A district mission manager was made in charge for each activity so that the work continued smoothly. All the district mission managers including Ms. Shalini Jain, and Ms. Nikha Sachan worked with enthusiasm.

Five milk producers and cattle rearers were selected from each block. All the information was provided to them in a meeting with the departmental officers. The 183 women selected in the group for dairy were sent on a study tour to a good dairy in the district.

Thirty people were sent to a good dairy outside the district. Three hundred women were sent to DRI (Deendayal Research Institute), Chitrakoot, for a three-day training.

Contact was established with renowned companies working in the field of dairy and help for milk production and sale was taken from them. Cooperation was taken by contacting and communicating with Namaste India (Kanpur), Paras Dairy (Bulandshahr), Gyan Dairy (Lucknow), Shyam Dairy (Prayagraj), Raj Dairy (Bindki, Fatehpur), Krishna Dairy (Ghatampur, Kanpur Dehat), Niba Dairy (Ghatampur), Ekta Dairy (Kanpur) Narayan Dairy (Kanpur), and Namo Dairy (Ghatampur). Discussions were also continued with the subject experts of dairy.

By providing necessary information to the women milk producers, their dairy business was increased by giving all kinds of support, which increased their income and morale and they became powerful by gaining knowledge.

A new program to increase income from neem was started. Indian Farmers Fertilizer Cooperative (IFFCO) requires neem seeds (Nimboli) for neem-coated urea. This new scheme was explained in the group meetings of 427 group friends. Nimboli was collected through the group from the neem tree available in the village. IFFCO made arrangements to buy it at the block level. IFFCO distributed 40,000 big neem trees to a group of 8 blocks. On 27 December 2020, an awareness campaign was conducted by inviting 700 beneficiaries. Shri Yogendra Kumar, Director, Marketing IFFCO, and members participated in it. Shri V. K. Singh, popularly known as 'Neem Man' also participated in it. It was inaugurated by Shri Vibhash Ranjan, Mission Director, Plantation from Lucknow. I received the 'Neemratna' award for two consecutive years. This new and unique experiment was very effective as the cost was negligible.

निबौली बेचकर आमदनी बढ़ा सकेंगे महिला समूह : राज्यमंत्री

बांदा : गोष्ठी को संबोधित करते जिलाधिकारी हीरा लाल। फोटो एसएनबी

मेडिकल कालेज प्रेक्षागृह में संगोष्ठी को संबोधित करते हुए बोले राज्यमंत्री

बांदा (एसएनबी)। महिला समूहों की आय बढ़ाने के लिए पांच प्रोजेक्ट जनपद में लागू किये गये हैं। नीम की निबौली महिला समूह बेचकर अपनी-अपनी आमदनी बढ़ा सकेंगी। यह बात राज्यमंत्री कृषि, कृषि शिक्षा तथा अनुसंधान लाखन सिंह राजपूत ने राज्य ग्रामीण आजीविका मिशन तथा इंडियन फारमर्स फर्टिलाइजर कोऑपरेटिव लिमिटेड बांदा द्वारा राजकीय मेडिकल कालेज के प्रेक्षागृह में नीमगुण, उपयोग एवं लाभ सम्बन्धी संगोष्ठी को सम्बोधित करते हुए कही। उन्होंने कहा कि किसान परम्परागत खेती को छोड़कर नयी तकनीक अपनायें जिससे वह अपनी आमदनी दोगुनी कर सकें। श्री राजपूत ने कहा कि नीम एक आयुर्वेदिक औषधि है। राज्यमंत्री कृषि श्री राजपूत ने कहा कि जनपद बांदा में पांच हजार महिला समूह कार्यरत हैं और इन गरीब महिलाओं की आमदनी बढ़ाने के लिए जिला प्रशासन द्वारा प्रभावी प्रयास किये जा रहे हैं, यह बहुत ही सराहनीय प्रयास है तथा जिला प्रशासन पंडित दीनदयाल उपाध्याय जी के सपनों को साकार करने का कार्य कर रहा है।

जिलाधिकारी हीरा लाल ने संगोष्ठी को सम्बोधित करते हुए कहा कि इस कार्यक्रम का उद्देश्य यह है कि समूह की महिलायें नीम से जुड़कर समृद्ध बनें। डीएम ने कहा कि इफ्को द्वारा नीम की निबौली की खरीद की जायेगी तथा जनपद में अप्रैल से निबौली खरीद की व्यवस्था कर दी जायेगी। जिलाधिकारी ने कहा कि जिला प्रशासन द्वारा ग्रामीण महिलाओं की आमदनी बढ़ाने के लिए पांच प्रोजेक्टों पर कार्य कराया जा रहा है। 1680 महिला समूह को मुर्गी पालन व्यवसाय से जोड़ा गया है। ग्लोबल नीम आर्गनाइजेशन द्वारा जिलाधिकारी को नीम रत्न का पुरस्कार प्रदान किया गया है। विपणन निदेशक योगेन्द्र कुमार ने कहा कि नीम संजीवनी है तथा नीम में सभी रोगों को हरण करने की क्षमता है, इसलिए आप लोग नीम के अभियान में जुड़ें तथा नीम के पेड़ों का अधिक से अधिक संवर्धन करें। इफ्को ग्रामीण जीवन के उत्थान तथा किसानों की आमदनी बढ़ाने के लिए लगातार कार्य करता रहा है तथा इफ्को के प्रयास से किसानों की 20 से 25 प्रतिशत आमदनी बढ़ी है। नीम मैन/अध्यक्ष ग्लोबल नीम आर्गनाइजेशन वीके सिंह ने गोष्ठी को सम्बोधित करते हुए कहा कि अमेरिका ने नीम का पेटेन्ट करा लिया था किन्तु हमारी संस्था ने नीम के पेटेन्ट को खत्म कराया। उन्होंने कहा कि नीम के प्रयोग से विभिन्न बीमारियों से बचा जा सकता है। इफ्को द्वारा नीम की निबौलियाँ 15 ₹ प्रति किलो खरीदी जायेंगी। संस्थापक पीपल नीम अभियान डॉ. धर्मेन्द्र कुमार ने गोष्ठी को सम्बोधित करते हुए कहा कि नीम बहुत ही लाभदायक है। नीम के दातून से जहां हम एक ओर अपने दांतों को साफ करते हैं, वहीं दूसरी ओर नीम का रस दवा का कार्य करता है। राज्य विपणन निदेशक इफ्को श्री अखिलेश सिंह ने गोष्ठी को सम्बोधित करते हुए कहा कि इफ्को किसान और कृषि की उन्नति के लिए लगातार कार्य कर रहा है। इफ्को किसानों के चेहरे पर मुस्कान लाने का कार्य करती है। इफ्को बुंदेलखण्ड क्षेत्र में निबौली की खरीद के माध्यम से महिलाओं की आमदनी बढ़ाने के लिए कार्य प्रारम्भ करेगी। मुख्य विकास अधिकारी हरिशचन्द्र वर्मा ने संगोष्ठी के अंत में अतिथियों का आभार व्यक्त करते हुए कहा कि दक्षिण भारत में नीम के बाग लगाये जा रहे हैं। इसी प्रकार हमें भी नीम के अधिक से अधिक पेड़ लगाने चाहिए। संगोष्ठी का संचालन उपायुक्त ग्रामीण आजीविका मिशन करुणाकर पाण्डेय ने किया। संगोष्ठी में उप निदेशक कृषि एके सिंह, उप निदेशक सूचना भूपेन्द्र सिंह यादव, सहायक निबंधक सहकारिता वीरेन्द्र बाबू, इफ्को तथा सहकारिता विभाग के अधिकारी तथा बड़ी संख्या में महिला समूहों की सदस्य उपस्थित रहीं।

The Bundelkhand Women Empowerment Broiler Farming Scheme of the Veterinary Department was implemented through a women's group. Each woman had to build a small poultry farm in her house and raise poultry. So, they were given money, training, chicks—all under the scheme. At the local level, they were sent to the poultry farming sites and given practical training so that they could learn by seeing and discussing on the location. Shri Akhilesh Sachan, Veterinary Officer, took interest in this work.

For the sale of eggs and meat, all support was provided to the beneficiary by contacting and communicating with wholesale poultry vendors located in Banda. For the first time in the state, Banda implemented this scheme through Livelihood Group.

Banda has a good variety of agricultural products. Organic, tasty and nutritious agricultural products like tur, desi jaggery of Naraini, gram, etc., are found in abundance in Banda. Women's groups were motivated and made aware for their trading. For this, all the information was given through training. The women who were already working in this field were motivated further. This increased their income with the same investment. Naraini Block Group also installed two machines so that the value addition could be increased by processing. I inaugurated the same on World Oilseeds Day, 2020.

The women of the group were given three days residential training at Deendayal Entrepreneurship Development Research Institute, Chitrakoot. Mr Sujit Kumar, Mission Director arranged the money from Livelihood Mission Lucknow for this. The women liked it very much. They saw and learnt a lot. It was a unique experience for the women who went out of the district for the first time.

Under Fit India and Yogmai Banda campaign, three to four women from each village were given training in yoga. These yoga-trained women taught yoga to people in their village. Due to this, people became health conscious and practiced yoga, with the result that their health improved. Women and women's groups were made conscious and alert regarding health. Yogacharyas Shri Ramesh Singh Rajput and Shri Ramesh Singh Patel did a good job by giving training.

Income, knowledge, and morale were increased with new experiments in women's development. This brought a feeling of joy.

महिला किसानों ने देखी वाराणसी की उन्नतशील बागवानी

जागरण संवाददाता, बांदा : उद्यान विभाग की ओर से जिले की समूह से जुड़ी 47 महिला किसानों को भारतीय सब्जी अनुसंधान संस्थान वाराणसी का भ्रमण कराया गया। वहां महिलाओं ने सब्जी की खेती की तकनीकी जानकारी हासिल की। टमाटर के कलम का रोपण कर उससे होने वाले लाभ की जानकारी ली।

जिला उद्यान अधिकारी परवेज खां व एनआरएलएम की जिला समन्वयक निशा सचान की अगुवाई में महिला किसानों का दल तीन दिवसीय दौरे पर वाराणसी गया है। यहां संस्थान द्वारा तैयार की गई परवल के प्रजातियों से कृषकों को अवगत कराया गया। सिंघाड़े की खेती व कमल की खेती करने के भी गुर सीखे। डा.डीआर भारद्वाज ने किसानों को बाजार के रुख को भांपकर शाकभाजी की खेती करने की सलाह दी। कद्दू वर्गीय सब्जियों के गुणवत्तायुक्त उत्पादन के बारे में तकनीक सिखाई। इस दौरान महिलाओं ने संस्थान में तैयार हो रही विभिन्न किस्म की बागवानी भी देखी। डीएचओ परवेज खां ने बताया कि समूह की इन महिला किसानों को विभाग की ओर से किराया, खाना आदि की व्यवस्था की गई है। यह महिला अन्य किसानों को भी प्रेरित करेंगी।

भारतीय सब्जी अनुसंधान संस्थान वाराणसी में बागवानी व सब्जी खेती देखती उद्यान विभाग की ओर से जिले से भ्रमण पर गई समूह की महिला किसान • जागरण

All these activities increased the knowledge, self-confidence, and enthusiasm of women. They got along well with each other. They started moving forward with increased knowledge and morale. The Hon'ble Chief Minister and the Hon'ble Governor were delighted to see their work and congratulated them.

❑

4.

Model Village

I became the District Magistrate of Banda on 31 August 2018 and on 24 February 2020, my tenure as the district magistrate of Banda came to an end. On 27 July 2020, Mr. Praveen Mahendra, a resident of Ambedkar Nagar sent me a WhatsApp message:

"Sir, the effort made by you in Banda under the administrative set-up is certainly exemplary for the whole country. It is our sincere wish that you must apply for the Prime Minister's Award. Regards, Mahendra."

I saw the message and forgot about it. Again, on 31 July 2020, Shri Mahendra sent a 10-page guideline for the Prime Minister's Award. I read it and found that I am actually eligible and this is where the story of Model Village started. I did not know Mr. Mahendra. So, I asked for his introduction. He told me that he had come to Banda on 28, 29, and 30th January, 2019 for the Start-up and Innovation convention. The convention was wonderful. Since then, Mr. Mahendra constantly observed my work on social media. Upon seeing my work, he inspired and encouraged me by sending me a message on the phone to apply. Upon his request, I made up my mind to apply.

This application was to be prepared in English. I spoke to Mr Arpit Gupta of Elets because the Start-up and Innovations convention had been managed by him. While I was talking to

Mr. Arpit Gupta, my old acquaintance, Mr Saurabh Lal, arrived. Mr Saurabh had created a website about Lucknow. We discussed it and he told me that he is a content writer. He had an eight-year-old company in Mumbai. I discussed this application with him. Mr. Saurabh Lal read the complete guidelines and said that we could apply and it was decided that we should apply for multiple areas. We applied for six areas:

1. Water conservation
2. Prison reform
3. Lok Sabha election campaign—2019
4. Malnutrition
5. Start-up and innovation
6. Administrative reforms

We applied, but it was not easy to collect all the information for the above. But gradually we collected information. Our team at Banda felt good that Banda could get the award for the work done by them. A lot of hard work went into this for about 2 months and all the information was collected. We analyzed the information; the numbers were eye-opening as to how well the work was done and achieved the pretty good results. But we did not know and did not even have the data as there is no practice in the district administration to prepare and learn about such statistics. The Prime Minister's Award application format had columns for statistics and results. It was a great pleasure to see the statistics of many projects and I felt good. If the result is not proved by data, then people consider it as mere talk and a sham, and the success of the work cannot be verified.

The application was first evaluated, and we were selected for the water conservation category. Subsequently, 2 officers were nominated. In this second level evaluation, the nominated officers had to visit the location to assess the ground reality of the work done in Banda. But due to the Corona epidemic, it was decided that online verification of all should be done, and then online verification took place. We got selected in the second level evaluation, too. The evaluation of the third level was done by adding the numbers of the first and second levels. For the third level evaluation, an online presentation and quiz were to be completed in front of four Joint Secretary level officers under the chairmanship of the Additional Secretary. That was awesome, too. We got the highest marks in all the three levels, and I stood first. Despite being a topper in level three assessment, I was suddenly dropped from the list without being given any reason. The presentation was to be made before the Cabinet Secretary at the fourth and final level. The reason was given that at the time of application, only the Collector posted in Banda could apply. I was not a Collector in Banda at the time of applying. This reason was not given in writing; it was given orally. There was no such instruction in the application. It was a big blow for me. After being the topper in the water conservation work in the whole country, the hope of getting the award for Banda had increased. Banda MP Shri R. K. Singh Patel was also very happy that his area would get an award for good work and would be recognized. Against this, applications were made at many levels including the Cabinet Secretary. On the information of the deletion, the MP himself and other MPs also wrote to the Prime Minister, Cabinet Secretary and Hon'ble Mr. Jitendra Singh, Minister, DARPG that it was wrong; if the application was invalid, it should have been rejected at the first stage itself. I personally went to Delhi and met Hon'ble Minister Mr. Jitendra Singh and the then Secretary, DARPG, but it was in vain. This troubled me a lot. I fought this battle at different levels for almost a month. Ultimately, I lost the battle. I was hurt at not winning the award. The way the name was dropped from the fourth level assessment was painful. The distress that arose in my mind remained for a long time. The statistics constantly reminded me of good work and failure to get the award for long haunted me.

In the meantime, I came to know about the Stockholm International Water Institute. I already had all the information and statistics; so, I applied there, too. My motive was to publicize this good work internationally. Some people would know about this good work through this application.

Voter turnout increased by about 10.55 per cent in the Lok Sabha elections, this strengthened our democracy. When the water level went up by about 1.34 meters, it reduced the problem of water. The increase in agricultural productivity by about 18.5 per cent increased the income of people. The results of reducing malnutrition are very pleasing. NITI Aayog has mentioned this in its report, 2019, on page number 73. We got the award for being number one in prison reforms. The results of the work done for farmers, students, youth, women—everybody—proved to be encouraging and beneficial. Many innovative steps like removing plastic, saving trees, etc., gave a new identity to entire Banda at the state and country level because of its good work.

I posted all these innovative results on my social media account on LinkedIn. Mr. Saurabh Singh, head of ICICI Foundation wrote a nice comment. He said that he saw my work on social media. I had done a good job in Banda as District Magistrate, it should be implemented in the state and other places, too. I informed Shri Munish, retired Chief General Manager, NABARD about this. Munishji talked to Saurabhji about how to implement Banda's work as a programme. Munishji took Saurabh Lalji on his team. A project was created and sent to the foundation. After several rounds of talks and deliberations, the Model Village program took shape. Since the program is based on the work done by me, he requested me to be part of it as an Honorary Consultant and I accepted. The process of taking admission in D.Litt. was going on and the concept of Model Village was the subject of my D.Litt. research. This also became another reason to join the Model Village. Munishji is the Honorary President of this model. He has experience of more than 34 years.

Model Village is getting its benefit. Shri Saurabh Singh's passion and devotion to rural development are unparalleled.

The most important thing is his ability to work and identify people. Recognizing the unique experiment in Banda on social media and deciding to implement it in a systematic manner is in itself a hallmark of the good person that Mr. Saurabh Singh is. In collaboration with the Foundation, Chief Executive Officer of Model Village Mr. Saurabh Lal and his team Mr. Sachin Choudhary, Mr. Raghavendra, Mr. Priyendra, and Mr. Kulwant run this entire program with the help of technology. The Model Village is progressing at its own pace with the cooperation of the Foundation's COO Mr. Anuj Agarwal, Finance Officer Mr Vineet and their team.

The three pillars of a model village

1. Village manifesto
2. Changemakers
3. Farmer producer company

1. **Village manifesto:** It talks about what is development, and how many development issues there are; it is a medium to create the urge for development in the mind of every villager. This will give information to the villagers about their development and will create a consensus for village welfare. The village will develop with the participation and support of all the people.
2. **Changemaker:** A changemaker is a local person from the same village who solves a social problem in a creative way. Changemakers will develop the village by undertaking social and positive welfare work with the zeal to innovate. He will be available 24×7 to the village for guidance and help.
3. **Farmer Producer Company (FPC):** A Farmer Producer Company is a group of farmers, who are actually engaged in agricultural production work and have a common belief in carrying out agricultural business activities together. Farmers

from one village or a group of villages can also form a FPC. The farmers in the village will form and run FPC themselves. They will convert farming from loss making into profit making activity through FPC. The villagers will be the owners of the company.

TheSouthAsianTimes.info HOLISTIC HEALTH September 11-17, 2021

Approaching the Tipping Point

By Bhaswati Bhattacharya

[illegible]

It is not money but mindset that is needed to catapult Traditional Bharatiya Sciences such as Ayurveda into the mainstream.

[illegible]

DEVELOPMENT

New Dawn of Rural Transformation

[illegible]

Model Gaon is inspired by Dr. Heera Lal, a senior IAS officer posted in UP.

राष्ट्रीय सहारा

12 नई दिल्ली। शुक्रवार • 25 जून • 2021

आईएएस, जो जगा रहा मॉडल गांव की अलख

> गांव को खुशहाल और ग्रामीणों को स्वावलंबी बनाने की डॉ. हीरालाल की अनूठी पहल
>
> मॉडल गांव का अंतिम लक्ष्य गांव में एक ऐसा नेतृत्व खड़ा करना है जो संपूर्ण गांव को स्वावलंबी बना सके

■ रोशन

नई दिल्ली। एसएनबी

गांव को खुशहाल और ग्रामीणों को स्वावलंबी बनाने के लिए एक आईएएस मॉडल गांव की अलख जगा रहा है। गांव साफ-सुथरे हों, कृषि लाभकारी हो, स्कूल उत्तम गुणवत्ता के हों, कृषि को व्यवसाय से जोड़ा जाए या जल संरक्षण हो, उत्तर प्रदेश कैडर के आईएएस अधिकारी डॉ. हीरालाल ने एक नया प्रयोग शुरू किया, जो अब परवान चढ़ता दिख रहा है। मॉडल गांव से अनेक प्रधान युवा और किसान जुड़े हैं। मॉडल गांव का अंतिम लक्ष्य गांव में एक ऐसा नेतृत्व खड़ा करना है, जो संपूर्ण गांव को स्वावलंबी बना सके।

मॉडल गांव की परिकल्पना के पीछे डॉ. हीरालाल बताते हैं कि अगस्त 2018 में जब बांदा जिले के डीएम थे, तो उन्होंने सोचा कि गांव का विकास अकेले सरकार नहीं कर सकती है। इसलिए उन्होंने ग्रामीणों को जोड़ना शुरू किया और उनके सामने एक एजेंडा रखा। उन्होंने जल संरक्षण का प्रयास किया और बांदा जिले का भूमिगत जल स्तर 1.3 मीटर बढ़ा दिया। बांदा जिले में सुधार से वह उत्तर प्रदेश का नंबर एक जिला बन गया। कृषि कार्य व्यवसाय और कृषि पर्यटन से जुड़ा, तो किसान नई तरह की खेती करने लगे और मुनाफा कमाने लगे। बांदा जिले में उनके द्वारा किए जा रहे कार्यों को देखते हुए आईसीआईसीआई फाउंडेशन ने उनके कार्य को समर्थन देना शुरू किया। उनके साथ सेवानिवृत्त अधिकारी मनीष गंगवार जुड़े और बांदा से शुरू हुई यह अलख उत्तर प्रदेश के और गांव तक पहुंच गई।

डॉ. हीरालाल, आईएएस

डॉ. हीरालाल इस वक्त उत्तर प्रदेश के नेशनल हेल्थ मिशन में अतिरिक्त मिशन डायरेक्टर हैं। अपनी जिम्मेदारी के अलावा वह मॉडल गांव के माध्यम से गांव का विकास कर रहे हैं। मॉडल गांव ने नवनिर्वाचित प्रधानों से संपर्क साधा है। कई प्रधान इस मुहिम में जुड़ गए हैं। मॉडल गांव का 25 सूत्रीय एजेंडा है। जो भी इसमें शामिल होना चाहता है, उन्हें इस एजेंडे के तहत काम करना होता है और मॉडल गांव उन्हें तकनीकी जानकारी एवं उनका हौसला अफजाई करता है। इस योजना के तहत हर गांव में 25 लोगों को नेतृत्व के लिए तैयार किया जा रहा है, जो गांव के बाकी लोगों को प्रेरित करें और उन्हें गांव के समग्र विकास एवं ग्रामीणों को स्वावलंबी बनाने के लिए प्रेरित कर सकें। नीति आयोग ने मॉडल गांव की सफलता को देखते हुए जिसे अपने एजेंडे में शामिल कर लिया है और अपनी वेबसाइट पर चढ़ा दिया है। नीति आयोग के उपाध्यक्ष डॉ. राजीव कुमार ने मॉडल गांव की परिक्रमा करने वाले डॉक्टर हीरालाल और उनकी टीम की भूरी-भूरी प्रशंसा की है।

Niti Aayog chief praises UP IAS officer for his effort to develop model villages

Neha.Lalchandani
@timesgroup.com

Lucknow: Niti Aayog vice-chairperson Rajiv Kumar has complemented UP IAS officer Heera Lal, additional director, National Health Mission, for his work to turn backward rural areas into model villages through public participation.

In a tweet on Wednesday, Kumar said: "IAS officer Heera Lal's endeavour to convert rural and downtrodden villages of Uttar Pradesh into 'Model Villages' through active public participation is a tremendous step. Ground work like this is important for India's holistic development. Great work!"

Heera Lal is additional director National Health Mission

Lal, who as district magistrate of Banda earlier, had carried out similar projects on water conservation, said that he was thrilled to have the work of NGO 'Model Gaon' recognised.

"The project was conceptualised by Munish Gangwar, retired chief general manager of NABARD. We started the project in January this year and already, 1,500 village manifestos, outlining how the locals would like to develop their village and what facilities they would like to have there, have been made. We are approaching newly elected pradhans, farmer producer organisations. Nehru Yuva Kendra members and asking them to join the effort," said Lal, who is an advisor to Model Gaon.

Lal said that his work in Banda while he was DM inspired Gangwar to take up the project at a macro level. In Banda, he said, his administration followed a bottom up approach in implementing water conservation schemes, increasing crop productivity etc, through direct involvement of residents in these projects.

"We have an example of a village pradhan from Gorakhpur who won the recent panchayat elections on the basis of a model village manifesto. We are now in the process of collaborating with him to help in the implementation of the manifesto which will see villagers come together for water conservation, creation of farmer producer companies to protect interest of farmers etc," he said.

11:03 AM | 3.7KB/s
Following
Rajiv Kumar
@RajivKumar1
Vice Chairman @NITIAayog | Economist, Author who loves Sufi music & Sahaja yoga meditation | Views are personal
Delhi India
niti.gov.in
Joined June 2012
514 Following
76.5K Followers
Followed by Dileep Pandey,BJP,UP, दिलीप पाण्डेय BJP, Emily Andre, and 249 others
Tweets
Tweets & replies
Media
Likes
Rajiv Kumar @RajivKumar1 · 10m
IAS officer @heeralalias endeavour to convert rural & downtrodden villages of #UttarPradesh into 'Model Villages' through active public participation is a tremendous step. Ground work like this is important for India's holistic development. Great work!
modelgaon.org/en/
4
6
20

❑

5.

Memorable Events

FIR: An incident took place in Banda district. A sitting MLA of the ruling party beat up the district official. We received information about it in the presence of the DIG and SP in NIC. We decided that if we did not get the FIR registered, then it would be difficult to run the administration in the district and the district officials will be demoralized. This information was sent to the higher officials. The FIR was registered as per the orders received from the higher officials. Though this decision looked simple, it was very complicated. Taking this decision at the district level and getting everyone's consent and implementing it was a very difficult task.

Popularity: My popularity continues even after moving out because my working style was based on public participation. I have always worked among people. I served them by being one of them. This approach is rarely seen in government officials.

Self-satisfaction: I got the realization of the results after moving from there.

Whether it is about the progress made in the complex water problem of Banda or the increase in agricultural productivity, whether village heads being in constant contact with me or the calls and messages that I still receive from the general public—I will be always grateful for so much affection that I have received from the people of Banda and this is the biggest reason for my contentment.

The Model Village program is continuing based on the results of more than 20 innovations done in Banda. This work is amazing. I feel happy with the increasing acceptance of the concept of Model Village.

❑

Summary

We should not underestimate most of our less educated public representatives, village heads, members, etc.

They are less educated, but they are learned and have gained worldly knowledge and experience, many times more than us. In the practical world, experience and social knowledge are more useful than bookish knowledge. We cannot do as much good work as a public representative can do among the people at the local level. Considering ourselves to be more knowledgeable, we do not give importance to the people's representatives and underestimate them. This only harms us. Public representatives and local officials are two sides of the same coin. Both are incomplete without each other. We are like the front two wheels of a cart. The biggest mistake of the bureaucracy in a democracy is not to give importance to the public representatives on any basis whatsoever.

The common people of the village, who are illiterate, should not be underestimated. They have more experience, contentment, courage, a spirit of sacrifice and native knowledge than us. It is their strength, which we neither understand nor use it. We make the mistake of underestimating and ignoring them. We should not do this.

PM, CM and DM are the three main posts in this country. The first two posts make plans and policies. The third post implements the plans and policies on the ground. The post of DM has a huge responsibility. On one side, the general public of the district is connected to it, and on the other side are the governments of the state and the country. This post is tied and tightened by the rope of expectations from all sides. Everyone expects administration like the Ram Rajya from the DM. There is a lot of pressure on him. There are many problems in front of him. It is not easy to work by striking a balance between problems and expectations.

It is the work of the district magistrate to take and implement decisions in public interest by balancing two mutually conflicting possibilities/activities simultaneously. Listen to everyone, do what your mind says, that what is right according to the rules and in the public interest. Winning the trust of the people is the biggest success. The job of the District Magistrate is to provide leadership to all. Generally, the district magistrate only provides leadership to the government machinery. I provided leadership to all the private and government organizations present on the soil of Banda and took everyone along in a team spirit. Everyone's participation, everyone's respect—that was my campaign. Under this leadership style, the people were ahead, and I was at the back. This increased public participation, public assistance, public support and every work was done through people's participation.

There is a gap between the public and the district administration. The public is afraid and hesitant to approach officials. Government machinery should work by going and staying among the people. We should work through the use of indigenous and local dress, language and food. I conducted most of the meetings sitting on the rug on the floor. I kept flowers, frills and gimmicky activities away. I met the public as if I was a member of their family. It is my way to form a family bond with them and become close within a minute to the visitor. Connecting with the public should be our main objective. I connected with the common man by making 3C – Connection, Communication and Cooperation. 3C is my main weapons.

I met everyone, big or small, educated and illiterate, and constantly learnt from them. After learning, I applied it. I also propagated the name from whom I learnt so that people would continue to teach and tell us in the future. Generally, officers take credit by claiming the good work done by others as their own.

We have abandoned our old strong traditions, customs, etc., considering them as insignificant and weak, whereas the situation is the opposite. I revived and established all such old, durable, strong things and traditions such as wells, ponds, plates and bowls made of leaves, earthenware, local cultural programs, local dress, food and drink.

I harnessed the power of love. The work that can be accomplished with love cannot be accomplished with sticks and punishments. I gave everyone a lot of time off. In the Lok Sabha elections—2019, too, the officials took a lot of leave, which is not usually the case. Non-availability of leave to government employees is a big problem. Officers show off their power by not granting due leave to the employees.

Along with leadership, we have to keep giving solutions to everyone's problems continuously. It is our moral responsibility to provide a positive and fearless environment to all. Our biggest strength is to keep learning continuously, keeping everyone together, working hard and being on time. Continuous reading increases your strength and makes you think like a rocket scientist.

Making decisions, completing every day's tasks on the same day and trying to implement the idea of accomplishing each task in a new way makes you stand out from the crowd. You shine. In a short span of time, you gain a name. Man has a desire to earn a name and money. The money is nothing in front of the honour and power of the name. The desire to earn a name by doing good work is the biggest capital.

We adopted three new methods and techniques in each project: First, we have to work with the money and resources available in the district. We won't ask for anything extra. Second, by taking along all the people related to the work together, by coordinating all the people, getting the work done by all and getting the active participation and ownership by all the people concerned so that people cooperate considering it as their own work. Third, to undertake activities, programs, measures, and efforts which is either low cost or no cost.

I worked as a servant, keeping away from official frills and pretentiousness. I went among the people in a simple way and not with the thought of being an administrator and ruler. We are not rulers or administrators, we are servants— this attitude should always be maintained.

It is generally seen that after joining the services, people stop studying or they do not have an interest. They do not like to attend training to get information. This makes their knowledge out of date and irrelevant. Knowledge is power. So, we should always maintain a close relationship with education and training. It gives us all kinds of power. After joining the services, I did my MPA from Syracuse University, New York, USA, and a PhD from Dr A P J Abdul Kalam Technical University, Uttar Pradesh. I am pursuing my DLitt from Dr Ram Manohar Lohia Avadh University, Ayodhya.

The intoxication of power and authority is very bad. Both of these happen with the post of DM. I always felt weak as DM because we were constantly battling with the problems and miseries of the people and were not able to solve them. I was addicted to alleviating the problems of the people, increasing their happiness and improving their standard of living. People often taunt that the IAS are 'black British'. I broke this notion and bridged the gap between the government and the society, working in the desi dress and speaking the local language to be desi DM. I rose above the thinking of the ruler-administrator and took the common man along and started to increase the prosperity and development of common man. The gist of the book is as follows:

Gist

1. Winning public trust should be our top most priority.
2. Adoption and promotion of local attire, cuisine, language and cultural activities.
3. Giving importance to the rich experience and information of the less educated and common people and adopting them.
4. To develop the ability to get things done with power of love instead of power of punishment.
5. Keep learning continuously.
6. Achieving success by working with public participation and available resources.
7. Bridging the gap between the government and society.
8. Taking quick decisions and solving problems amicably.
9. Trying to perform each task in a new way to do the same thing differently.
10. We are not rulers and administrators but public servants. We should always work with this thought.
11. Stay away from the ego of position and power and its intoxication. Be simple, humble and empathetic.

साइकिल रैली से दिया सुपोषण का संदेश

सैकड़ों छात्राओं ने शहर में जगाई अलख, साइकिल चलाकर डीएम हीरालाल ने किया नेतृत्व

डीएम ने मंडप में पहुंच वर–वधू को दिया आशीर्वाद

पौधारोपण को बढ़ावा देने के लिए चला रहे पेड़ प्रसाद अभियान

जागरण संवाददाता, बांदा : पौधारोपण को बढ़ावा देने के लिए डीएम हीरा लाल पेड़ प्रसाद अभियान चला रहे हैं। साथ ही शादी-ब्याह में वह हरियाली के लिए लोगों को प्रोत्साहित कर रहे हैं। शुकुल कुआं स्थित एक विवाह समारोह में वह सोमवार को पहुंच गए। यहां वर-वधू को आशीर्वाद दिया और पेड़ों की सुरक्षा के लिए प्रेरित किया।

डीएम मंदिर, मस्जिद, गुरुद्वारा और चर्च सहित हर धार्मिक व वैवाहिक समारोह में हरियाली बढ़ाने को पौधे वितरित करा रहे हैं। अभी तक वह एक लाख से ज्यादा फूल व औषधीय पौधों का वितरण करा चुके हैं। रविवार की रात इंदिरा नगर निवासी सुरेश कुमार गुप्ता की बेटी ज्योति गुप्ता का ब्याह समारोह था। यहां बरातियों के लिए गमले सहित करीब डेढ़ सौ पौधों का वितरण किया गया। पौधों के प्रति लोगों को उत्साहित करने के लिए डीएम, वन व उद्यान विभाग की टीम के साथ बरात में पहुंचे। उन्होंने वर-वधू दोनों को आशीर्वाद दिया। साथ ही पेड़ पौधों के महत्व के बारे में जानकारी दी। कहा कि जीवन का अस्तित्व पेड़ पौधों के बिना संभव नहीं है। डीएफओ संजय अग्रवाल, सदर तहसीलदार अवधेश कुमार निगम, सेवानिवृत्त सीडीओ हीरा लाल, प्रशंसा गुप्ता, जुनैद मौजूद रहे।

शहर के शुकुल कुआं स्थित मैरिज हाल में पौधों के साथ डीएम हीरा लाल (बीच में) तथा दूल्हा पुष्पक (बाएं) व दुल्हन ज्योति (दाएं) • जागरण

राजधानी में धाक — बांदा डीएम हीरालाल ने साझा की चुनाव से संबंधित जानकारियां, सेंटर ऑफ पालिसी रिसर्च में बांदा के अभियान की गूंज

दिल्ली के मंच पर साझा हुआ 90 प्लस अभियान

अमर उजाला ब्यूरो

बांदा। लोकसभा चुनाव में मतदान के प्रति मतदाताओं का रुझान बढ़ाने के लिए यहां चलाई गई 90 प्लस मुहिम राष्ट्रीय स्तर पर चर्चा में है। मंगलवार को दिल्ली में आयोजित कार्यक्रम में यह मुख्य मुद्दा रही। मुहिम के अगुवा डीएम हीरालाल इस कार्यक्रम में बुलाए गए थे। उन्होंने अभियान संचालन की विस्तृत जानकारियां दीं।

दिल्ली के सेंटर ऑफ पालिसी रिसर्च संगठन के तत्वावधान में आयोजित गोष्ठी में मतदान के प्रति लोगों की सहभागिता को बढ़ाने पर मंथन किया गया। इसमें उपस्थित डीएम हीरा लाल ने पिछले लोकसभा चुनाव में बांदा में जोरशोर से चलाए गए 90 प्लस अभियान का हवाला देकर कहा कि मतदाताओं के दिलोदिमाग में यह भाव जगाना जरूरी है कि उनके एक वोट से कितना बदलाव आ सकता है।

उन्होंने कहा कि भले ही 90 फीसदी का लक्ष्य पूरा नहीं हो पाया, लेकिन मतदान में 11 फीसदी का इजाफा हुआ। खास बात यह भी रही कि दिव्यांगों ने पहली बार बड़ी संख्या में मतदान किया। उनके 85.35 फीसदी वोट पड़े।

दिल्ली में आयोजित बैठक में भाग लेते बांदा डीएम हीरालाल।

अभियान में दिव्यांगों का मतदान बढ़ाने के लिए भी विशेष कवायदें की गई थीं।

डीएम ने वो तमाम जानकारियां शेयर कीं जो 90 प्लस अभियान में यहां डीएलओ से लेकर विभिन्न विभागों के कर्मचारियों, अधिकारियों ने अपनाई थीं। टीमें मतदाताओं से घुलमिलकर उन्हें मतदान के लिए प्रेरित करती रहीं। मतदान केंद्रों में छांव, पानी, स्वल्पाहार, सांस्कृतिक कार्यक्रमों की व्यवस्थाएं की गईं। डीएम ने कहा कि मतदान का ग्राफ बढ़ाने के लिए मतदाताओं को विश्वास में लेना बेहद जरूरी है। उनके मन में जो नकारात्मक चीजें हैं उन्हें दूर करना होगा।

सेंटर ऑफ पॉलिसी रिसर्च की अध्यक्ष यामिनी अय्यर ने इस अभियान और प्रयासों को सराहनीय और उदाहरण बताया। कहा कि देश के अन्य जनपदों में भी ऐसे ही प्रयास किए जाने चाहिए। उन्होंने बांदा के अभियान को मॉडल के रूप में सोशल मीडिया से लेकर राष्ट्रीय मीडिया तक प्रचारित किए जाने पर जोर दिया।

पीएम ने 90 प्लस अभियान को सराहा

कृषि विश्वविद्यालय में मौजूद एडीजी एसएन सांबत, डीआईजी एके राय, डीएम हीरालाल आदि। अमर उजाला

अमर उजाला ब्यूरो

बांदा। डीएम हीरालाल के नेतृत्व में बांदा जिले में चल रहे 90 प्लस मतदान अभियान को प्रधानमंत्री नरेंद्र मोदी ने सराहा। अपने भाषण की शुरुआत में ही उन्होंने कहा कि यहां के जिले के अधिकारी 100 फीसदी वोटिंग के लिए मेहनत कर रहे हैं। उन्हें मैं बधाई देता हूं। वास्तव में सरकारी मशीनरी द्वारा किया जाने वाला यह काम बधाई देने योग्य है। ये राजनीति से परे होकर काम कर रहे हैं। निर्वाचन आयोग को ऐसे अफसरों को देखना चाहिए। उनके अनुभवों को आगे आने वाले चुनाव में इस्तेमाल किया जा सकता है। प्रधानमंत्री द्वारा सार्वजनिक मंच से बांदा में चल रहे 90 प्लस मतदान मिशन की सराहना करने पर इस अभियान के अगुवा जिला निर्वाचन अधिकारी हीरा लाल ने कहा कि यह पूरी टीम के लिए खुशी की बात है।

प्रशासन और पुलिस अफसर रहे आसपास

आदर्श आचार संहिता के चलते प्रशासन और पुलिस के वरिष्ठ अधिकारी प्रधानमंत्री के मंच या सभास्थल पर तो नहीं गए, लेकिन उनकी व्यवस्थाओं और सुरक्षा की पल-पल जानकारी या खबर रखने के लिए सभास्थल के नजदीक कृषि विश्वविद्यालय भवन में मौजूद रहे। अपर पुलिस महानिदेशक (इलाहाबाद जोन) एसएन सांबत, कमिश्नर शरद कुमार सिंह, डीआईजी एके राय, डीएम हीरालाल, एसपी गणेश प्रसाद साहा आदि मौजूद थे। उधर, अपर एसपी एलबीके पाल सहित कई जनपदों से आए आईपीएस, पीपीएस अफसर ड्यूटी पर तैनात रहे। उधर, सभा स्थल पर बांदा, हमीरपुर, फतेहपुर, महोबा, चित्रकूट जिले के भाजपा नेता बड़ी संख्या में उपस्थित रहे। पूर्व जिलाध्यक्ष बालमुकुंद शुक्ला, हमीरपुर लोकसभा प्रभारी पुरुषोत्तम पांडेय, पूर्व जिलाध्यक्ष लवलेश गुप्ता, पूर्व विधायक राजकुमार शिवहरे, वंदना गुप्ता, अल्पसंख्यक मोर्चा क्षेत्रीय महामंत्री मुनीर खां, आरिफ खां, रामरतन कुशवाहा, संजय दुबे, अरुण पाठक, अशोक जाटव आदि शामिल रहे। ब्यूरो

डीएम ने दिए जिला व तहसील स्तरीय अधिकारियों को निर्देश

मिट्टी के कुल्हड़ों में ही चाय पियेंगे अधिकारी व कर्मचारी

जागरण संवाददाता, बांदा : अधिकारी हो या कर्मचारी अथवा उनके दफ्तरों में आने-जाने वाला कोई आगंतुक अब अब सरकारी कार्यालयों में मिट्टी के कुल्हड़ में ही चाय पीते नजर आएंगे। जिलाधिकारी ने प्लास्टिक के प्लेट व गिलासों पर प्रतिबंध लगाते हुए मिट्टी के कुल्हड़ों का उपयोग करने के निर्देश सभी जिला, तहसील व ब्लाक स्तरीय अफसरों को दिए हैं। उन्होंने कहा है कि इसका सख्ती से अनुपालन कराया जाए।

बढ़ते प्रदूषण को देखते हुए शासन ने पालीथिन के साथ प्लास्टिक के कप-प्लेट व गिलासों पर भी रोक लगाई है। लेकिन इनका उपयोग अभी भी धड़ल्ले से हो रहा है। इन पर प्रभावी ढंग से रोक लगाने के लिए जिलाधिकारी ने सख्त तेवर अख्तियार किए हैं। उन्होंने सभी जिला स्तरीय अफसरों को निर्देश दिए हैं कि दफ्तरों में हर हाल में कुल्हड़ों का प्रयोग किया जाए। शासन की मंशा है कि दशक भर से तकरीबन ठप हो चुकी कुम्हारी कला फिर जीवित हो। कुल्हड़ों का उपयोग होने से जनपद के युवाओं को रोजगार मिलेगा। वहीं कुम्हारी कला से जुड़े परिवारों की आय बढ़ेगी। साथ ही पर्यावरण में भी सुधार होगा। डीएम ने आदेश की प्रति पुलिस अधीक्षक, अपर जिलाधिकारी, नगर मजिस्ट्रेट व प्रभारी अधिकारी संयुक्त कार्यालय को भी भेजा है। कहा है कि कार्यालयों में आगंतुकों एवं अधिकारियों व कर्मचारियों को स्वल्पाहार के समय प्लास्टिक के स्थान पर चाय-पानी के लिए कुल्हड़ उपयोग में लाए जाएं।

जिले में भले ही प्लास्टिक पर प्रतिबंध न लगा हो लेकिन जिलाधिकारी ने सरकारी कार्यालयों में आदेश भेज अपने इरादे स्पष्ट कर दिए हैं।

कुल्हड़ में चाय • जागरण

"इस नई पहल से जहां पर्यावरण का संरक्षण होगा, वहीं रोजगार के अवसर भी बढ़ेंगे। सरकारी दफ्तरों में इसका अनुपालन कराने को कहा गया है। कहीं लापरवाही मिली या आदेश की अनदेखी हुई तो कार्रवाई भी की जाएगी।
हीरालाल, जिलाधिकारी।

अंतिम सांसें गिन रहा कुल्हड़ का व्यवसाय

बढ़ते प्लास्टिक के चलन से जनपद में कुल्हड़ का व्यवसाय अंतिम सांसें गिन रहा है। दस साल पहले जिले में करीब 300 परिवार कुम्हारी कला से जुड़े थे। लेकिन मौजूदा में महज 36 परिवार ही इस पेशे को जीवित किए हैं। शादी-ब्याह हो या होटल-दुकानों में सभी जगह प्लास्टिक की प्लेटें, गिलास आदि का इस्तेमाल होता है। यह सस्ता होने की वजह से ज्यादा चलन में है। यदि डीएम के इस फरमान पर अमल हुआ तो कुम्हारी कला के दिन फिर बहुरेंगे। कुम्हारी कला से जुड़े शहर के [illegible] ने बताया कि अब सिर्फ दीपावली व कुछ गिने-चुने त्योहारों में ही कुल्हड़ व दीपक की बिक्री होती है।

डीएम साहब नहीं, हम तुम्हारे काका हैं बेटवा

मतदान लक्ष्य हासिल करने के लिए पिपरी गांव को लिया गोद, नन्ही ज्योति के गीतों पर हुए मोहित

छात्राओं ने जागरूकता रैली में दिखाया दम, गूंजे नारे

वाट्सएप पर संदेश भेजकर आमंत्रित किए जाएंगे बाहरी मतदाता

डीएम बंगले की खाली पड़ी जमीन में मिनी फॉर्म हाउस से जीरो बजट खेती सिखाएंगे, बारिश की बूंदे ही रचेंगी बुंदेलखंड

बंगले को बना दिया खेती की 'पाठशाला'

इनसे सीखें

आवासों में 200 एकड़ जमीन बेकार पड़ी

किसानों के लिए खेती से जुड़ी हर चीज होगी

अब हस्ताक्षर होगा उपस्थिति का प्रमाण

परिषदीय विद्यालयों की मनमानी रोकने को नई कार्ययोजना, कारगर साबित हो सकता है यह प्लान

बांदा डीएम की अनूठी पहल

यह होंगी खास बातें

Greeting, Appreciation and Congratulation Messages

I am very happy to know that the book Dynamic D.M. is being published by you based on your specific work related to social service. During your posting as the district magistrate in Banda district, remarkable programs like 'Start-up Summit Innovation', and the 'Save well and pond' campaign during summer to deal with the water crisis were well conducted. Your readiness and eagerness to help the public regarding water conservation in Banda are commendable. Your ability to solve problems with public participation is remarkable.

I hope that the publication of the book Dynamic D.M. will prove to be a milestone for the readers.

I extend my best wishes for the success of its publication.

—RAJIV KUMAR
President, RERA

Noteworthy programs like 'start-up innovation Summit' in Banda district, '90 plus per cent' awareness campaign to increase voting percentage, yoga programs as a daily routine in jail, and the 'Save well and pond' campaign during summer to deal with water crisis were well conducted by District Magistrate Dr. Heera Lal.

Dr. Heera Lal, District Magistrate, Banda has carved a unique identity for himself in Banda district as a competent and efficient administrative officer. He has made a significant contribution to eradicating malnutrition and the Anna System in the district and developing Kalinjar Fort as a tourist destination, as well as successfully implementing the schemes, programs and priorities of the state government in the district.

I wish him a bright future.

—Dr Anup Chandra Pandey, IAS

Ex-Chief Secretary, Uttar Pradesh

The Indian Administrative Service (IAS) is one of the most prestigious administrative services in the country, which is determined to continuously serve a country like India which has a massive democracy and social diversity. Since 75 per cent of the country's population resides in villages, the development of villages is the foundation of the country. The responsibility of the officers of the Indian Administrative Service towards rural development becomes very important.

It has often been felt that over the years, there has been a lack of coordination between the administration and the citizens, mainly due to the workload, paucity of time and new problems arising every day. But it is only in such circumstances that the capabilities of an officer develop and he starts looking for a way to solve the problems of the people through innovative ideas.

Dr. Heera Lal is an IAS officer who tries to find solutions to the toughest problems in difficult situations. He has the ability to solve problems with the participation of his subordinate officers/ personnel and common citizens. I have seen him working as district magistrate in Banda, where he solved the problems of the citizens with their participation, for which he received praise from the regional and central level officers as well as the local village heads.

In the book Dynamic DM, Dr. Heera Lal shares his long administrative experience, which is exemplary, with his peers, subordinates and future generations who will join the administrative services. I congratulate Dr Heera Lal for his conscientiousness and for providing suitable services and my best wishes are with him that he will continue to serve the public with full devotion in the future as well.

—Alok Sinha, IAS
Agricultural Production Commissioner
Govt. of UP

The book captures various problems solved by a district magistrate. It also presents the problems faced during the administration of our districts. Some of the problems are social whereas some are infrastructural. But all the problems cannot be solved without policy-level interventions. That is the most interesting part of the problem-solving aspect captured in this book. DM Heera Lal makes efforts to solve the problems with a minimal budget by involving the community. We can term it as social approach in district problem-solving.

Some of the problems (which definitely will be found interesting by the readers) solved by DM Heera Lal need a special mention. Banda is a district in UP which has been hit by severe droughts for many years now. This has led to a drastic fall in the groundwater level. Over the years, many plans and interventions were tried, but there was no breakthrough. Heera Lal during his stint as district magistrate involved the community and brought about a social movement to revive wells and ponds. This led to a magical transformation with considerable rise in the groundwater level and recharging of wells along with ponds.

Another achievement which needs attention is the communication campaign to increase the voting percentage in the district. It is a true story of social marketing and creative persuasion by mobilising all the state government departments.

Finally, this book captures the struggle of Dr. Heera Lal in childhood. This makes it a great motivational read for the youngsters who may get frustrated due to a lack of resources in their lives.

I wish this book great success and hope it will be a valuable asset to administrative colleges, policy makers and IAS aspirants.

My best wishes to Dr. Heera Lal for continuing his hard work with creative execution. I hope to read more stories from him in the near future.

— Prof. Devashish Das
Gupta Professor, IIM Lucknow, UP

I am very happy to know that a book Dynamic D.M. is being published about the social service projects implemented by you. While participating in a program regarding water conservation in Banda, I have personally experienced how prepared and eager you are to help the public. You have an amazing ability to solve the problems with the participation of the public.

I not only hope but have full faith that the readers will get a lot of inspiration and learn from the publication of this book. I convey my best wishes for the book Dynamic D.M.

—Late Raju Srivastava
Comedian and Chairman,
Uttar Pradesh Film Development Council

I am extremely happy to know that a book is going to be published on the life struggles of Dr. Heera Lal and his experiences as DM of Banda.

I am familiar with Dr. Heera Lal since he was the district magistrate of Banda in 2019 although our Satna is a district in MP and Banda is in UP. But if the admiration for the work of an administrative officer crosses the border of the state and reaches the neighbouring state, then it can be called an achievement of that administrative officer.

There may be five to six hundred districts in the country where many IAS officers are DMs. In Satna district itself, I have been familiar with almost all the collectors since the 1990s, but most of them followed a set pattern. Only one or two of them left their mark among the common people.

The rest of them limited themselves to bungalows and offices. They had nothing to do with the common people.

Just by looking at the manuscript of Dr. Heera Lal's book Dynamic D.M., one knows that his path resembles that of Kabir's *(Jo Ghar Phoonke Aapno Chale Hamare Saath)*, the path of encountering contradictions, which is not possible for everybody to follow.

This is the path of such people who contemplate about the country, the world and the society. After occupying such an important position, they see the extreme poverty of the people. They fight contradictions and disorders.

I am 77 years old now. But till date, I have not forgotten an essay by Acharya Ramchand Shukla which I had read in childhood, in which he said that whether you put a gourd in a well, pond or sea, it will stay above the water. Thus, talented people make their mark everywhere.

This quote by Acharya Shukla is fully applicable to IAS Dr. Heera Lal.

Whether he was a district magistrate in Banda, a deputy collector or a municipal commissioner—wherever he worked—he carved a different identity. On the one hand, he made a place among the oppressed, victimized and neglected people, and wherever he saw contradictions or atrocities being committed against the poor, he always stood against it.

Officers in such positions are always faced with situations where influential people put pressure on them and make their leadership a medium of plundering. Various conspiracies are also hatched against honest officers and this is even more common in a state like UP, where the powerful mafia and mighty people dominate every field, indirectly. But even in such a state, the way Dr. Heera Lal has made his place among the public without bothering about them is praiseworthy. His concept of 'Model Village' is such that its fame has crossed the boundaries of the country and has reached abroad.

It is an old tradition to write a biography. Some writers have written their biographies, but it has been useful for others.

This book (Dynamic D.M.) based on the life of Dr. Heera Lal is also very interesting and exemplary; it is co-authored by Mrs. Kumud Verma.

I have full faith that this book will prove to be a guide for other determined district officers who do not bow down to injustice and all other officers.

—Padma Shree Babulal Dahiya
Satna (MP)

I met Heera Lal when I joined Maxwell School of Public Administration and Citizenship, Syracuse University, USA, to do a diploma course in Public Administration. I was there to escape the rigours of officialdom while Heera Lal wanted to pursue his goal of doing master's in the same discipline. Two things struck me when I got to know him as a fellow student—his dynamism and commitment to whatever he chose to do. Though senior by many years in age and service, he took me under his wings and became my friend, philosopher and guide. The year was 2010. I was not very well versed in social media and efficient use of computers, while he was an expert in both. He patiently taught me whatever skills I needed to complete the course without any mishaps. Sad to say that despite his best efforts, I failed to become an ardent user of social media.

Heera Lal was aware of the many things that can be achieved through positive and effective use of this new media. He was full of ideas as to how social media could be used to clean up the government machinery and make it responsive to the needs of the people, shows his commitment to responsibilities entrusted to him. Be it the initiative of addressing and solving issues related to availability and use of the scarce resource of water or conduct of elections to promoting yoga for ensuring the health and well-being of people of Banda district. He addressed issues that needed to be solved to create a society that took care of the infrastructure and basic needs of the people—pioneering efforts in afforestation, social forestry, nutritional needs of children, farmers' welfare, waste management leading to increased use of biodegradable and environmental-friendly materials, etc. Many of his efforts were recognized not just within the district or the state, but also at the national level. Acknowledgement of the model village concept by NITI Aayog is in itself a recognition of his acumen.

Heera Lal is a dynamic, action-oriented officer for whom working with dedication for improving the life of the people is at the core of his personality. He doesn't miss any opportunity towards meeting this and creates opportunities where none is evident. The book says it all. The accolades are richly deserved. He's indeed 'DYNAMIC'.

—Sheela Thomas, *IAS (Retd.)*
Kerala

If an administrative officer is determined, he can change the image of any area. Whether it is about making the most backward district like Banda of Bundelkhand plastic-free, or solving the water crisis, or women empowerment, or even taking the benefits of various government schemes to the real beneficiary, this document describing successful methods of implementation by Dr. Heera Lal is inspirational and exemplary for the administrative officers and common people of the country.

—Lieutenant Colonel Yuvraj Malik
Director, National Book Trust

The journey of a village boy to become a district magistrate is inspiring. Innovative works done by IAS Dr. Heera Lal will show a way to many.

—Swami Mitrananda
Chinmaya Mission, Chennai

Dynamic DM depicts the journey of a bureaucrat who is dedicated to making a difference in the lives of many people in the backward district of Banda. Banda, which had been plagued by many adversities, such as water scarcity, perennial drought and malnutrition, as well as deforestation, underwent a complete transformation under the leadership of Dr. Heera Lal. The book vividly depicts how, after taking over as DM, Dr. Heera Lal began to solve these pressing challenges one by one, bringing the district into the development mainstream. This journey from experience in the field to expression in the book is captivating. His 'Model Gaon' initiative, which was inspired by Dr Kalam's PURA (Providing Urban Amenities to Rural Areas) mission, has been a game-changer for rural India, providing a holistic model of development. I hope this book and the ideas serve as the source of inspiration for young officers in the years to come.

—Srijan Pal Singh
CEO, Dr A. P. J. Abdul Kalam Centre
Former Adviser to
Ex-President of India Dr Kalam

A good and conscious effort for rural development despite the limitations of administration: an extraordinary and commendable effort from an ordinary position.

—Prof. Anil Gupta (Retd.)
IIM, Ahmedabad

Dynamic D.M. is an interesting documentation of contemporary history and response to challenges.

Dr. Heera Lal is a doer who leads by example. Banda was transformed under his guidance and leadership. Interventions relating to water, doubling the farmer's income, jail reform and environmental protection reflect complete out-of-the-box thinking. The book will be an invaluable guide towards contributing to practical inputs from the grassroots level for development.

—Dr Gursharan Dhanjal
Managing Editor & Editor
SKOCH Group

Dynamic D.M.

The responsibility and opportunities for change that a district collector or district magistrate possesses are probably unparalleled at any other level of government. At a time when we lament the absence of 'convergence' between diverse efforts of line departments, the district as a unit is probably the best place for this convergence to find reflection. However, leadership matters. Experience is testament to the fact that visionary and dynamic leadership at the district level can usher in a long-lasting change.

Despite the centrality of water to the existence of life, we have treated this resource with scant respect. As adverse weather events become the norm, the threat to sustained availability of safe water is one of the foremost challenges we face. In this context, the seeds of change sown in Banda district by Dr. Heera Lal assume great significance.

Dr. Heera Lal realised that water does not follow traditional administrative boundaries—either on the surface or beneath the ground. He also knew that attempts to address this issue through the narrow lens of individual line departments would not provide solutions. Financial resources were not the primary constraint. Most importantly, Dr. Heera Lal recognised that water conservation required the winning of hearts and minds of the people. Unless communities are inspired to participate and take action, change is not possible.

The success of the efforts in Banda are not limited to investments made or the number of water conservation structures created, or water conservation structures revived. The success of Dr Heera Lal's effort is in his ability to have made water everyone's business in the district. He did so fearlessly and with a single-mindedness, using local language, idiom, culture and traditions as a part of the story to inspire people.

We live at a time when 'hope' is important. The efforts in Banda by Dr. Heera Lal fill us with hope and optimism.

—V K Madhavan
CEO, Water Aid India

I am happy to know that Dr. Heera Lal's autobiography Dynamic D.M. is going to be published. Leadership is not only a magnet, it also generates a large and attractive force by combining scattered iron molecules in a particular direction and adding them in a sequence and then the iron molecules become a great force without destroying each other's energy.

While working as the DM of Banda district, he did the same with enthusiasm. On 6 October and 8 December 2018, both of us launched a water conservation campaign by involving citizens and organizations of the entire district, making the district water abundant. Later, he took it forward. Similarly, his achievements in other areas were also reward-oriented. This devotion of Dr. Heera Lal will become a source of inspiration for future district magistrates.

Jal Guru

—Mahendra Modi, IPS DGP (Retd.)
Water Conservation Adviser (UP)

I am indeed honoured to write a few lines on Dr. Heera Lal's book Dynamic D.M. Having interacted with many district magistrates throughout my career as a development professional, it is with immense respect that I acknowledge and admire the multi-dimensional role of a district magistrate and the wide range of development issues that a DM has to provide leadership on, as Dr. Heera Lal profiles in his book. These issues range from ensuring access to sanitation and drinking water, improving nutrition outcomes, water conservation, education, environmental and waste management issues, raising the profile of the district and many more such issues. Dr. Heera Lal, as a dynamic DM in Banda, provided leadership on these many issues and his book profiles his journey, the challenges he faced and the impact and positive transformation his work brought about in the lives of the community. Dr. Heera Lal has built on this wide-ranging experience to develop the concept of 'Model Gaon', highlighting the importance of integrated development to improve the overall quality of life in rural India. May his book serve as an inspiration to those who aspire for a career of service and contribution to transformational and sustainable change in our villages.

My very best wishes for a successful publication of your book.

We are also grateful for your immense support and guidance for our work and look forward to your continued support.

—Tinni Sawhney
Chief Executive Officer
Aga Khan Foundation India

It has often been felt that over the years, there has been a lack of coordination between the administration and the citizens, mainly due to the workload, paucity of time and new problems arising every day. But it is only in such circumstances that the capabilities of an officer develop, and he starts looking for a way to solve the problems of the people through innovative ideas.

Dr. Heera Lal is an IAS officer who tries to find solutions to the toughest problems in difficult situations. He has the ability to solve problems with the participation of his subordinate officers/ personnel and common citizens. I have seen him working as district magistrate in Banda, where he solved the problems of the citizens with their participation, for which he received praise from the regional and central level officers as well as the local heads.

I congratulate Dr. Heera Lal for his diligence and delivering good services and I send my best wishes that he will continue to serve the people with all his heart in the future, too. With my best wishes.

—Mukul Singal, IAS
President, UP IAS Association

I had the opportunity to see the work of Dr. Heera Lal when I went to the district jail, Banda in 2019 to research the jails of Uttar Pradesh and under the Tinka-Tinka prison campaign. I saw him as a very energetic and completely dedicated bureaucrat. Some things seemed very inspiring. For example, I saw him making a list of the tasks for the entire day and working on giving a shape to the model of development. He has a tremendous ability to self-assess his work by casting time and responsibilities in one mould. He also built a pond at the back of his house for water conservation. He appeared serious and alert about the issues related to the land. He established a different kind of tradition in Banda of assessing the development work of that day with his officers and staff in a systematic meeting every evening. I also realized at that time that an outline was being formed in his mind about the all-round development of Banda jail. I may have some disagreements about his style of work, but overall, one can always see his dedication to work. I am happy to see that he is compiling his work now.

Such efforts are also commendable because usually, the final point of development reaches the people, but the journey of development often remains untouched. I congratulate him for forging his own path of action.

—Dr Vartika Nanda Founder
Tinka-Tinka Foundation Head,
Journalism Department Lady Shri Ram College,
University of Delhi

❑